THE HISTORY OF POOLESVILLE
[Maryland]

Dona L. Cuttler
and
Dorothy J. Elgin

HERITAGE BOOKS
2007

HERITAGE BOOKS

AN IMPRINT OF HERITAGE BOOKS, INC.

Books, CDs, and more—Worldwide

For our listing of thousands of titles see our website
at
www.HeritageBooks.com

Published 2007 by
HERITAGE BOOKS, INC.
Publishing Division
65 East Main Street
Westminster, Maryland 21157-5026

Other books by the author:

Montgomery Circuit Records, 1788-1988 [Maryland]

One Man's Family

Paperclips: Selected Clippings from The Montgomery Sentinel *[Maryland], 1900-1950*

The Cemeteries of Hyattstown [Maryland]

The Genealogical Companion to Rural Montgomery Cemeteries

The History of Barnesville and Sellman, Maryland
Dona Lou Cuttler and Ida Lu Brown

The History of Clarksburg, King's Valley, Purdum, Browningsville and Lewisdale [Md.]

The History of Dickerson, Mouth of Monocacy, Oakland Mills, and Sugarloaf Mountain

The History of Comus [Maryland]

The History of Hyattstown [Maryland]

International Standard Book Number: 978-0-7884-1450-3

This book is dedicated to

Charles William Elgin

1915 - 1997

He was important to Poolesville for many years,
caring for the town, the Monocacy Cemetery,
and was a source for much of the historical
information found in this book.

Acknowledgements

The authors wish to express their appreciation to Louise Ehlers for the cover art work and assistance preparing this book. Thanks also to Ida Lu Brown and Mary Hertel for their contributions of additional research, legwork and accommodations. For their help at the Montgomery County Historical Society, thanks to Jane Sween and Pat Anderson. And posthumously for the inordinate collection of facts, photographs, and records, thanks to Charles W. Elgin.

TABLE OF CONTENTS

PHOTOGRAPHIC CREDITS

Main Street, collection of Dorothy J. Elgin, p. 6
Camp Benton, collection of Mary Shaw Williams, p. 8
Axe Hendle Brigade, collection of Mary Shaw Williams, p. 9
Regimental Band, 20th Massachusetts, collection of Mary Shaw Williams, p. 9
Elijah V. White, collection of Montgomery County Historical Society, p. 12
Poolesville in 1862, collection of George Brackett, p. 20
Main Street, collection of Dorothy J. Elgin, p. 26
Snow Storm, collection of Dorothy J. Elgin, p. 27
Main Street, collection of Dorothy J. Elgin, p. 28
1905 Poolesville Baseball Team, collection of Dorothy J. Elgin, p. 29
1918 Poolesville Baseball Team, collection of Dorothy J. Elgin, p. 30
Poolesville Band, collection of Doris Matthews Lewis, pp. 30-31
Poolesville's First Telephone, D. Cuttler, p. 32
Telephone House, D. Cuttler, p. 33
C & P Building, D. Cuttler, p. 33
Poolesville Fire 1923, collection of Dr. Arthur F. Woodward, pp. 35-36
Town Hall, D. Cuttler, p. 38
Poolesville Postmark, collection of Dorothy J. Elgin, p. 39
Briarley Hall, collection of Dorothy J. Elgin, p. 42
Students and Faculty of Briarley Hall, collection of Dorothy J. Elgin, p. 43
Graduates of Briarley Hall, collection of Ida Lu Brown, p. 44
Briarley Hall Barracks, collection of Dorothy J. Elgin, p. 44
Military Drill, collection of Dorothy J. Elgin, p. 45
Study Hall, collection of Dorothy J. Elgin, p. 46
Football Team, collection of Dorothy J. Elgin, p. 47
Track Squad, collection of Dorothy J. Elgin, p. 48
1915 Baseball Team, collection of Dorothy J. Elgin, p. 49
1917 Baseball Team, collection of Dorothy J. Elgin, p. 50
Chiswell's Inheritance, collection of Dorothy J. Elgin, p. 50
Henry Davis House, D. Cuttler, p. 52
Elijah Methodist's Manse, D. Cuttler, p. 52
Elijah Methodist, D. Cuttler, p. 53
Love and Charity Hall, collection of Montgomery County Historical Society, p. 54
Harry M. Williams House, D. Cuttler p. 55
Benjamin White House, D. Cuttler, p. 56
Hodgson House, collection of Dorothy J. Elgin, p. 57
Dr. Elijah White House, D. Cuttler, p. 58
Julius Hall's Tenant House, collection of Dorothy J. Elgin, p. 59
Presbyterian Manse, collection of Dorothy J. Elgin, p. 60

CHAPTER ONE
THE EARLY HISTORY OF POOLESVILLE

Not far away, old Sugar Loaf rears lofty to the skies,
An through Montgomery's rolling fields the voice of beauty flies.
Not far away Potomac flows and the old canal's asleep,
and every garden has a rose and here the old dreams creep.

Old churches, gentle memories, schools, stores and over all
The fragrance of the old estates with stained and ivied wall.
Phantoms of wars long fought and done, the saber's gleam, the shot,
And shadows of old village folk none ever have forgot.

Oh, village 'mid the miles of wheat, the corn, the rye, the grass,
No longer through your ancient road the lumbering coaches pass;
But ever looking down on you the mountain guards your rest
Sweet Poolesville, with a rose to dream upon your quiet breast.
— Bentztown Bard

Poolesville began as virgin forest cleared by early settlers moving west from Anne Arundel and Prince George's County. Early land grants in the area of what is now Poolesville include "Killmain," "Forest," "Joseph's Choice," and "Elizabeth's Delight." When Daniel Carroll purchased "Killmain" in 1735 and Thomas and John Fletchall patented "Two Brothers" in 1737 the tracts were located in Potomac Hundred, Prince George's County. Hundreds were created as county divisions when an area reached one hundred taxables. Taxable persons were: All slaves over age sixteen, and all white males over sixteen, with the exception of paupers receiving alms and clergymen. Potomac Hundred had been created from Rock Creek Hundred in 1722. In 1728 Monocacy Hundred was created, which included all the land north of Seneca Creek. This area was wide open for land grants, and in 1741 this area was further divided into Seneca Hundred. In 1748 Prince George's County's taxables reached 6,624 and the General Assembly passed an act creating Frederick County on December 10. "Elizabeth's Delight was surveyed in 1753, resurveyed in 1759 for 498 acres patented to Charles Hoskinson. In 1754 Henry Wright Grubb patented 2,078 acres called "Forest" where the east side of Poolesville stands today. In 1758 Captain Joseph Newton Chiswell received a patent for 90 acres of the land grant "Joseph's Choice." In 1760 John Poole purchased part of "Elizabeth's Delight" from Charles Hoskinson paralleling the Chiswell land. The property was resurveyed and named "Poole's Right." "Difficulty" was resurveyed in 1765 for George Willson.

In 1776 the new independent politicians made it their first order of business to carve two new counties out of Frederick County. The lower area was named Montgomery, the first such county to be named for patriot. The families of John and Joseph Poole, John Dowden, John Fletchall, Hugh Hoskinson, Alexander Whitaker, James Soper, and Captain Solomon Stimpson were land owners in the area. As the population grew, Sugarland Hundred was created. Each hundred had a constable and was comparable to present election district designation.

The following men from the vicinity served in the American Revolution: 1st Company Upper Battalion Militia: George Hoskinson, [as a private, then, Ensign 16th Battalion, 1st Lt. Upper Battalion], Charles Hoskinson, Ensign Hugh Hoskinson, Patrick Money, Joseph Poole; 2nd Company Lower Battalion Militia: Zadock Lackland, Middle Battalion William Vinson; 3rd Company Upper Battalion Militia: Daniel Veirs, Elijah Veirs; 4th Company Upper Battalion Militia: James Aldridge, Edward Beeding, Henry Beeding, Joseph Beeding, Thomas Beeding, Abraham Fletchall, George W. Fletchall, Alexander McIntosh; 5th Company Middle Battalion Militia: Martin Fisher, Sr. [and provided wheat for military use]; 5th Company Lower Battalion Militia James McDonough, Samuel Beall White [also private in 1st Maryland Line, wounded at 2nd battle of Camden in the left kidney, abdomen, and back]; 6th Company Lower Battalion Militia: William Jones; 7th Company Upper Battalion Militia: John Poole II; 8th Company Upper Battalion Militia: Aeneas Campbell, Jr., James Campbell; Lower Battalion: James White [also served in 7th Maryland Line]; 16th Battalion: Major Aeneas Campbell, Sr., William Veirs; Captain John Fletchall died June 20, 1777. 3rd Maryland Line: Richard Hall, and Benjamin Poole.

The 1783 tax assessment lists the following:
"Difficulty" James Soper, 100 acres, one log dwelling house, 3 out buildings
"Forest" Josiah Harding, 170 acres, one dwelling house, two log houses
"Forest" George Blackmore, 100 acres one old dwelling house
"Johnny and Molly" Joseph N. Chiswell, 6 1/4 acres, one dwelling house
"Poole's Rectification" Joseph Poole, 70 acres, one log dwelling house, one
        kitchen; this was formerly "Elizabeth's Delight"
"Two Brothers" Alexander Whitaker, 200 acres, log dwelling, mill house
        Alexander Whitaker was the tax assessor for the area. He combined twelve of his tracts into this larger property. The log house was built c. 1740 and is the oldest house in the vicinity. The frontier area had settlers living on sparsely populated large tracts.
        Robert Peter purchased "Forest" from Henry Wright Grubb and had it re-surveyed in 1784. The "Resurvey on Part of Forest" contained 1,796 acres. On this property stands another of the early houses of the area. The one-room log house was built by John Poole, son of John c. 1793 and features a stone fireplace. Poole obtained a storekeeper's license in 1800 and operated the business from his

2

house adding the post office in 1810. The house faced what was then called John Wilcoxen's Road, later referred to as Coxen's Road. Joseph and Benjamin Poole opened a store at the crossroads and by 1800 there were four entrepreneurs in the village: John Poole, the merchant, George Powell, the shoemaker, Raphael Melton, the tailor and Aeneas Campbell, a cabinet maker and Justice of the Peace. In 1816 John Poole moved to Barnesville. Joseph Poole, John's uncle, purchased and subdivided his property into six lots. Two of his sons purchased one lot and Christian Hempstone built a store on one of the other lots. Farmers in the outlying areas began to frequent the growing community as a market center. It was also the voting place for Medley Election District.

In 1812 the United States of America had only been free of the British forces for twenty-nine years. They returned to invade what they had lost, and the citizens of Montgomery responded by raising an extra Brigade. Thomas F. W. Vinson served as Lieutenant and William Chiswell entered as a Corporal, both rose to the rank of Captain. Both men raised up a company of men by holding a barbecue on August 1, 1814. Knowing that Washington City was in eminent danger, the following men were some of the recruits mustered in that day: Sargent John A. Chiswell, Robert Dade, Samuel Darby, Lloyd F. Harding, Lt. James C. Lackland, William Poole, Sr., Thomas Reed, George Reed, William Reed, Richard P. Spates, Captain Turner Veirs, Charles A. Waters, Richard Waters, William O. West, Richard Wootton, Martin Fisher, Richard Higgins, Nathan Veirs, and Walter Williams. These men marched to Annapolis before proceeding to the disastrous Battle of Bladensburg. Lloyd F. Harding guarded the prisoners and James C. Lackland was taken prisoner by the British.

Of the regular army the Seventh Brigade 3rd Regiment under Lt. Colonel John Linthicum had officers from the area including: Major Joshua C. Higgins, Major Isaiah Nichols, Adjutant William Brewer, surgeon, Quartermaster Robert D. Dawson, Paymaster John J. W. Jones, Surgeon Grandison Catlett and Surgeon's Mate Colmore Williams. They saw action throughout the conflict, and were discharged in Baltimore.

Following the war Robert Peter subdivided the property inherited from his father, George, on Coxen's Road into lots in 1819. On March 16, 1827, Richard Lyles filed a petition to have the path of Coxen's Road altered. Claiming the road was on swampy ground the following petitioners requested that the road be moved beginning at William O. West's tavern [site of present Town Hall] as far as Henry Fowler's tavern: William O. West, George Graves, Ignatius P. Lyles, Daniel Trundle, Richard Lyles, John A. Howard, John M. Williams, Thomas T. Wheeler, Stephen Ramsburg, James Fletchall, and Stephen White. The following people objected to the course of the road being changed: Dennis Lackland, Richard P. Spates, Benjamin Poole, Nelson Fisher, Jeremiah Harbin, Thomas B. Benson, Hilleary T. Jarvis, and Richard Poole. When the roadbed was moved in 1829 the new course bisected the lands of George Peter, Ignatius Davis, and

3

Benjamin Poole. Davis and Poole had purchased their land from Dennis Lackland, explaining why they were opposed to the move. George Peters' lots were more accessible after the road was diverted, but the John Poole's properties were not, and none of the other lots were ever built on.

Some of the local men who served in the War of 1812 include: Elijah Veirs White, Benjamin White, George Chiswell, Edward Chiswell and Edward Wootton, surgeon.

In 1831 Samuel Mullen of Leesburg, Virginia was contracted for mail service. His route included Rockville, Darnestown, Dawsonville, Poolesville, Conrad's Ferry and Leesburg. He came through Poolesville weekly and held the position until 1835. He was paid $75.00 annually for his services.

In 1833 the Chesapeake and Ohio Canal opened. The area farmers now passed through Poolesville when taking produce to the canal and mills. Alexander Whitaker owned "Difficulty" a large tract of land which was divided into sixteen lots after his death. Each of his eight children inherited two lots, but none of them planned to use them for building. The lots were west of the town's center, resulting in a shift in building. Poolesville merchants stocked farm supplies and equipment and other tradesmen offered services such as carriage making, tailoring, smithing, shoe making, carpentry, millinery, wheelwrighting and coopery. A hotel, livery, tavern, doctors office and other conveniences were also available. the first physician was Dr. Lyles who resided just outside the town. Also located just outside of town was Joseph P. Collier's Mill. In 1845 it was sold to the Milfords and was known as Milford's Mill.

In 1840 the Medley District Agricultural Society was formed in Poolesville. Farms during this time period were largely self-sufficient, growing a variety of crops that the family would need for the year. Poolesville was the site of the first County Fair held on October 10, 1843. Prizes were offered for top breeds in farm animals, crop varieties, spinning and weaving examples and other handwork. In the Agriculture Society's report of 1849 the farmers shift to wheat and fertilizers indicates the decline of tobacco as the predominant crop. In the 1850's crop rotation improved agricultural practices in Montgomery County. Farmers specializing in grains and sold the crop at a profit for services and to buy seed for the next years' planting. Benjamin Shreve and Henry Young specialized in cattle, and Richard Henry Jones specialized in milk and butter. This was Poolesville's halcyon decade.

In 1848 Elijah Veirs White his home, "Stoney Castle," near Poolesville bound for Lima, New York. He enrolled in Lima Seminary at the age of 16 and after two years attended Granville College in Ohio. His tuition per term was $14.00 with the fall term beginning in September of 1850, and the spring term in February of 1851. He remained there until May of 1852. In 1855 "Lige," as he was known, went to Kansas to fight with a company of the Missouri Home Guards to battle abolitionists in the destiny of the state's position when it was admitted to

4

the Union. He returned to Poolesville in 1856 realizing innocent people were also being hurt in the border battles.

In 1851 a list of businessmen was compiled. It included merchants, hotel keepers and physicians in Poolesville. The merchants of dry goods, groceries and hardware were: Thomas Darnall & Isaac Young, Samuel C. Veirs, and Jesse T. Higgins whose brother, Darius, clerked for him. Dr. William Brewer, Dr. Nicholas Brewer, Dr. Lewis Fechtig, Dr. E. White, Russell Brace, and Dr. Thomas Poole were in practice at this time. Richard P. Spates was the hotel keeper. Samuel Milford, George Robertson and John Robertson were millers. Other businessmen included Philip Reed, cabinetmaker; Henry Collier, cabinetmaker; Mrs. E. J. Eldridge, milliner; Benjamin F. Reed, painter; Thomas Ashton, shoemaker; William Nokes, shoemaker; Edwin Cruit, saddler; Christian N. Mossburg, saddler; Joshua McDonough, wheelwright; William McDonough, wheelwright; Hileary Farmer, blacksmith; Samuel Cator, blacksmith; Richard P. Spates, blacksmith; Benjamin Cator, blacksmith; and five Hall tailors—John W., Joseph F., Thomas, Thomas R., and John R. Hall. The Halls also had a tin shop. Robert J. Groff was the school master.

If you had a house built in the mid-nineteenth century it would have likely been constructed by one of these local carpenters: Barnard T. Norris, Franklin Veirs, Charles W. Norris, John O. Merchant, Walter Williams, or Adam Yingling. The town hall was located on "Back Street" now called Wootton Avenue. The magistrate was Alexander Soper and Hilleary Hoskinson, Sr. was the constable.

Elijah Veirs White purchased a farm across the Potomac River in Loudoun County, Virginia in 1856. The river at this point is fordable, and White's Ford played a strategic role in the next decade. On December 8, 1857 he married Sarah Elizabeth Gott, daughter of M. Richard Jr. and Mary Elizabeth Trundle Gott. White then joined Captain Shreve's Company of Loudoun Cavalry.

In 1859 a meeting was called in Poolesville with Dr. William Brewer presiding in order for citizens to voice their opinion following the raid at Harper's Ferry. Twenty-four men were elected at the meeting to protect the area. They were given the authority to arrest suspicious people who could not account for the purpose of their activities in the vicinity. Also at the meeting a declaration of Southern sympathy was made against Northern aggression.

The population approached 200 in 1860, and the businesses included a tinsmith, George McIntosh; blacksmiths Lemuel Beall, James L. Beall, Francis Ross, Larry Edward, Samuel Cator, George D. Powell, Richard P. Spates, and Joseph N. Chiswell; wheelwrights Warren Boliger, Oliver Anderson, Dawes Norris, and Joshua McDonough; livery stables were run by mechanics Barnard T. Norris, John T. Norris, Charles W. Norris, John Smith, and James L. Norris. Thomas McDonough was a horse breeder. General stores were operated by Thomas Rudolph Hall, Benjamin S. White, and Jesse T. Higgins with Daniel E.

Heffner and Robert T. Hempstone, clerks. Barbers had a chair in the store or on the porch. Tavern keepers were Michael Connelly and William O. West. The millinery shop sold hats fashioned by Angelina Nicholls. The hotel offered rooms where salesman could stay while peddling their wares. The tailors were John R. Hall, Cincinnatus Hall, and Benjamin Cator. Houses constructed during this time were built by Samuel Moulden and John O. Merchant who also built coffins. John Phillips was a plasterer, Edwin Cruit and Edward Hoskinson the saddlers, George W. Dawson a lawyer, James Sherwood, William Nokes, and D. H. Chamberlain the shoemakers, Benjamin F. Reid was a house painter and his father Philip Reid was a cabinetmaker. Physicians in the area were Joshua Hatcher, Russell Brace, and Charles Shreve. Poolesville was the second largest town in the county at this time.

Chapter Two
The Civil War Years

Following a meeting of the men of Poolesville in 1859 the following Resolution was passed: "That in view of the warlike attitude taken by the North against the South, we pledge our allegiance to the South in support of our constitutional rights, and that all we have of force and means shall be devoted, when required, to protect and defend Southern rights against the aggression of the North." Men in Montgomery County answered the call "to arms." The Poolesville Unit of the Maryland Militia was known as the "Poolesville Dragoons." Benjamin S. White led this light cavalry company.

Also in 1859 George W. Chiswell formed a band of volunteers calling themselves "Chiswell's Exiles" to protect the town from Union invaders. In 1929 while renovations were being made to the Julius Hall house in Poolesville, workman uncovered sabers wrapped in Baltimore newspapers dated 1859. The sabers were unused and obviously hidden from Union men who had been sent to Poolesville to break up the formation of the Poolesville CSA Company.

One of Poolesville's most notable sons was Corporal Elijah Veirs White who served in the Loudoun Cavalry and was transferred to Dr. Frank Mason's Company of Turner Ashby's 7th Virginia Cavalry. After the firing on Ft. Sumter off the peninsula of Charleston, South Carolina, the Confederate troops began to prepare for the Union forces to cross the Potomac River to enter Virginia.

The following men had volunteered their services for the confederate cause prior to the draft: farmers Joseph J. Benson, George W. Chiswell and Edward Jones Chiswell, overseer David Carlisle, farm laborer David Coberth, farmers Robert Dade and John O. Elgin, farm laborer James W. Eichelberger, Martin Fisher, clerk Alexander Fahey, Daniel S. Heffner, farmer Nathan L. Hoyle, overseer Andrew I. Hoskinson, farm laborer Richard Kuhn, overseer William Kingsbury, farmers William Matthews, Jr., James M. Matthews, Charles H. Matthews, Franklin Piles, Benjamin R. Poole, William Seneca Veirs, and Henry B. Veirs, merchant Benjamin S. White, farmers William C. White, Samuel White, Thomas H. White, John C. White, and William T. Young.

The Army of the Potomac had encampments in Poolesville for almost the entire duration of the Civil War. Poolesville provided good roads to the Potomac River ferries and fords, and is located near the "horseshoe bend" in the river, thus allowing numerous vantage points. Area farms such as the Williams farm off Westerly Road the Gott farm behind the Poolesville High School provided food for the troops.

Colonel Charles P. Stone sent an advanced guard from the "Rockville Expedition" in June of 1861. A detachment was left in Poolesville to string telegraph wires and guard the canal. The telegraph allowed the operator to maintain communication with Washington and to send and receive messages from the field. Thus, the dispatches were printed with Poolesville, Maryland as the heading, and were widely reprinted in newspapers of the day.

In July of 1861 Jesse T. Higgins, Poolesville merchant, was arrested for recruiting rebels. He was released after a hearing, but later imprisoned in the Old Capitol Prison. William T. Aud, a local farmer, was also imprisoned for his support of the Confederate forces.

The following regiments comprised 12,000 artillery, infantry and cavalry men encamped in and around Poolesville by August: 3rd New York, 42nd New York, 1st Minnesota, 15th Massachusetts, 20th Massachusetts, and 106th Pennsylvania. The Union Army established a signal station atop the town hall to relay messages from Darnestown to Sugarloaf Mountain's signal station. Colonel Edward D. Baker arrived in Poolesville in 1861 and made Frederick Poole's "1785 House" his headquarters. Here he planned an attack on the Confederate Forces now known as the Battle of Ball's Bluff. He supposedly remarked when asked about President Lincoln's call for 75,000 men for 90 days service "We will not need them for 90 days, we will wipe them out in 60 days."

One such encampment was Camp Benton located on the Charles McGill Williams farm several miles from Poolesville. It was named in honor of General Lander's friend and had ample clean water for the number of men. The 20th Massachusetts arrived first building a permanent camp including underground trenches to carry heat for the tents and a log hospital in which a large Thanksgiving Ball was held on September 25.

Over one hundred fifteen tents were pitched, some floored and having exterior walls. The logging detail provided materials for the headquarters, a notched log building in the Williams' wheat field.

The regimental band consisted of twenty-four musicians who were also trained in ambulance service and first aid. They not only provided music for the above mentioned ball, but also for dress parades, reviews and funerals. The camp also had a photograph salon, or tent with cameras and props. Men could pose and send pictures to loved ones back home.

In addition to drills, maneuvers, and military routines, the men at Camp Benton enjoyed athletic competition in the form of climbing a greased pole, catching a greased pig, sack races, and other sports. Men also were drilled in the accuracy of their firearms on the firing range located on the field beyond the camp.

The Nineteenth and Twentieth Massachusetts Regiments were camped near the Forty-Second New York and Seventh Michigan. The large concentration of men in one area necessitated infrastructure such as regular postal delivery, and cooking facilities. The bakery issued bread and biscuits to the men, and beans were also cooked daily. One dish described by a clerk was made with pork and hard bread, boiled in water and served like chowder.

By October 15, 1861 there were approximately 15,000 troops in and around Poolesville. General Stone sent the 15th Massachusetts to the Potomac River on October 20th to investigate a Confederate camp across from Harrison's Island. Other regiments were sent across the Potomac near Edward's Ferry toward Leesburg. Additional brigades under Colonel Edward D. Baker left Poolesville at 1 A.M. on October 21, meeting up with the 15th Massachusetts at Harrison's Island before crossing into Virginia. Confederate Commander General Nathaniel G. "Shanks" Evans sent the 8th Virginia, the 13th, 17th and 18th Mississippi, totaling 1,600 troops to meet Baker's forces of 2,000. Confederate spies signaled troop movements across the Potomac routinely.

Corporal "Lige" White was at his Loudoun County farm on leave and volunteered to help where ever he was needed. He was assigned to Colonel Eppa Hunton and served as a courier, scout, and guide. He assisted three Confederate units and earned commendations for his efforts.

Colonel Baker was killed almost instantly and each regiment fought for itself with no leader. The Rebs held the bluff as 921 men from the 42nd New York, 15th Massachusetts, 20th Massachusetts and 71st Pennsylvania were killed as they attempted to cross the Potomac River and climb the bluff. Among the wounded was First Lieutenant, Co. A, 20th Massachusetts Oliver Wendell Holmes, Jr. The Confederates lost only 149 men. General Stone was blamed for the chaos which ensued following the death of Colonel Baker. This led to the establishment of a Congressional Committee on the Conduct of the War. For lack of any one person to blame General Stone was arrested in February 1862 and jailed until August 16, 1862.

Camp Benton was struck and moved closer to the river. The removal of the tents and moveable items was extremely orderly. The buildings were abandoned and the labyrinth of underground heating tunnels must have looked odd without the camp. Several years later the regiments marched from the Potomac River toward Poolesville and recognized the site of Camp Benton, and Mr. Williams greeted them along the road.

Following the battle, recruits were being assigned the task of digging trenches in Leesburg and the the vicinity. In December of 1861 Captain "Lige" White opened a recruiting office in Leesburg to raise an independent company for border patrol and warfare. Fifteen chose his unit over digging trenches and became couriers from Winchester to Leesburg, Virginia. Others soon followed and a loosely organized group of Comanches took up position in Waterford, Virginia with the task of watching Point of Rocks and Brunswick along the Potomac River. They also gathered horses and wagons for the cause.

Occasionally the hot air balloon of the Union Army could be seen near Edwards Ferry. Thaddeus Lowe kept an eye on troop size and movements from the Maryland side of the Potomac as both armies settled down in their winter camps. From his birds eye view he was able to report details from Point of Rocks to Leesburg. Confederate forces practiced camouflage techniques to conceal their numbers and whereabouts.

Brigadier General John Sedgwick assumed command of the Union forces which spent the winter in Poolesville. Making winter quarters meant building structures to weather the cold and frosty Maryland nights. Several areas on the east side of town were used, as well as to the south. The men spent their days drilling, doing military maneuvers, and building earthworks along the Potomac River. Other activities included foraging through area farms for food and chopping wood for fires. This often included school desks, church pews and split rail fences of the locals. In February of 1862 the regiments of Poolesville were designated the Second Division of the Second Corps. The 11th New York Cavalry stayed in Poolesville when the others withdrew.

General Charles P. Stone established a camp for runaway slaves from Virginia in the vicinity of the present-day Jerusalem community. The camp eventually had small cabins according to Ora Lyles. Because Washington City's slaves had been freed, many blacks in Montgomery County headed for the District of Columbia, looking for the glow of a Union campfire as they traveled in darkness. Most were only passing through, and ended up in camps in Washington for the duration of the war.

Beside Thomas N. Gott's house in Poolesville the 14th New Hampshire set up camp. Twenty of the tents were for officers and support staff, and the remaining one hundred fourteen tents were for the enlisted men. Between the 14th New Hampshire and the 39th Massachusetts was a house used as a bakery. Nearby the 10th Massachusetts Battery was encamped behind the M. E. Church which was used as headquarters for the cavalry. The old school house was also pressed into service, with the signal corps tower located behind the cemetery of the church. Troop strength, positions and movements could be communicated from Sugarloaf Mountain and Darnestown's signal station.

Meanwhile the Rebel forces of White's men were officially organized during January of 1862. This included the enlisting and recording of troops as "White's Rebels." After capturing a lieutenant from the 28th Pennsylvania

Infantry, they saw a pontoon bridge being set up near Harper's Ferry for an invasion in February. By March the Confederate forces moved to the southern part of Virginia, and no longer had their home territory. They met up with Lieutenant Colonel Thomas Munford and the 2nd Virginia Cavalry. Munford organized the 250 or so men into a company. Elijah V. White was the Captain, Frank M. Myers 1st Lieutenant, William F. Barrett recruiting officer and 2nd Lieutenant, and R. C. Marlow 3rd Lieutenant and Quartermaster. During the spring of 1862 they practiced guerrilla warfare on the Union troops. Captain White was shot in the face and left the company for several weeks during his recuperation.

On June 20, 1862 following their artillery bow at Slaughter Mountain, four men arrived with news that "Chiswell's Exiles" would soon be joining their company. The men left Poolesville after cutting the telegraph wires, and crossed the Potomac River before sunrise on August 13. Their guide took them to Captain White. As more men joined in the coming months, this group formed Company B of the 35th Battalion.

COLONEL ELIJAH VEIRS WHITE

12

Officers of Co. B 35th Virginia Cavalry

Col. Elijah Veirs White, formerly of Poolesville
Capt. George White Chiswell of Poolesville
1st Lt. Joshua R. Crown of Adamstown
2nd Lt. Nicholas W. Dorsey of Urbana
3rd Lt. Edward J. Chiswell of Dickerson
Surgeon Edward Wootton of Poolesville
1st Sarg. Henry Sellman of Barnesville
2nd Sarg. John Henderson of Poolesville
3rd Sarg. John Scholl of Dickerson
4th Sarg. Charles Green
1st Corp. Frederick Williams of Poolesville
2nd Corp. Charles Scholl of Dickerson
Bugler Crome Phillips of Washington City

The men of Company B included the following names:

Robert M. Aldridge, died at Point Lookout prison on August 17, 1864
John W. Appleby, POW at Old Capitol Prison
Welsey Appleby, POW at Aiken's Landing
James Barnes, POW at Point Lookout
Lemuel Thomas Beall
R. M. Beall
William Beall
William Boswell
John P. Bouic
Charles M. Boyles
William H. Bozzell
Edward Brady
William Braddock
John Breathard, POW Ft. Delaware
John Brusnan, POW Elmira
James H. Burnhard
Charles M. Butler
George W. Butler
George W. Calhoun
Michael Cantwell
David G. Carlisle
William Carlisle, POW Old Capitol Prison
Christopher Columbus "Lum" Cecil of Comus, POW Ft. McHenry
Edward Jones Chiswell of Poolesville
George Walter Chiswell of Poolesville
William F. Chiswell of Poolesville
Patterson Clayes, POW Ft. Delaware

James Cochran, died while POW at Point Lookout 1864
David Coburth
John Croft
Frederick N. Crown
Frank H. Crown
John O. Crown, POW Ft. McHenry
Joshua R. Crown, POW Ft. McHenry
T. E. Cunningham, died in 1862
Lee M. Dade
Robert Dade, POW Ft. Delaware
William E. Darne, of Darnestown
William Davidson
James Davis, escaped from Ft. McHenry
John William Davison, POW Old Capitol Prison
Thomas Davison, POW Old Capitol Prison
William Harrison Dickerson of Dickerson
Nicholas W. Dorsey, captured at Monocacy June 16, 1863 POW Ft. McHenry
James E. Durham, POW Pt. Lookout
Charles W. Eader, captured at Potomac July 30, 1864 POW Elmira
Lewis A. Eader
John Ogilvie Elgin
William Fitch
Nicholas C. Fitzsimmon
Michael Fitzsimmons, captured at Potomac July 30, 1864 POW Elmira
James Frye
William Gallager
William F. Gatton, died in train wreck en route to Elmira July 18, 1864
Eugene Giddings, POW Old Capitol Prison
John Gordon, POW Old Capitol Prison
William Curran Graham
William Gray
Charles Green, POW Ft. McHenry
C. P. Green, POW Old Capitol Prison
G. P. Green, POW
Abraham Harding
William D. Hartley
Thomas Harwood
William T. Harwood, POW Old Capitol Prison
Richard Poole Hays of Barnesville
Samuel Brook Hays of Barnesville
Stephen Hefner of Poolesville
George Henderson

John Herbert
William Herbert
W. Hickley
John William Holland, POW Old Capitol Prison
James H. Hoskins, POW Ft. Delaware
William H. Hubbard, POW Ft. McHenry
Samuel Jarboe of Edwards Ferry
Benjamin John Jones
J. W. Kephart
William H. H. Kessler
Daniel Key, POW Old Capitol Prison
John Kraft
George A. Lamar
James E. Lowry
James W. McCormick
Bernard F. McGlone, POW Ft. Delaware
Henry McNeil
Joseph Magaha
William P. Martin
Charles W. Matthews of Poolesville, POW Elmira
James M. Matthews of Poolesville
John Maxwell
John Moiner
George Morris, POW Pt. Lookout
John Morris, POW Pt. Lookout
Elias Moulden of Poolesville
Archibald Mulligan
Lewis Needhammer
James Nolan, POW Old Capitol Prison
Charles O'Boyle, POW Pt. Lookout
James O'Boyle
William Oden
John Ordman, POW Ft. McHenry
Henry Orme of Barnesville
Lindley Orme of Barnesville
Joseph C. P. Peter
Tom Peter
William T. Peters, POW Ft. McHenry,
John Phillips, POW Old Capitol Prison
Elias Price of Poolesville, wounded at Brandy Station, right leg amputated
Benjamin Franklin Pyles of Beallsville
M. Thomas Pyles of Beallsville

James W. Reed of Poolesville
John M. Robinson
Samuel Ryan, POW Ft. Delaware
Charles E. Scholl of Dickerson
John H. Scholl of Dickerson
Alonzo Sellman of Barnesville
Henry C. Sellman of Barnesville
Wallace Sellman of Barnesville
William F. Sheehan
William Sherman
Daniel Trundle Shreve of near Dickerson
Edward Simpson
Charles W. Smith
Jesse Rice Smith
Richard S. P. Stallings, POW Pt. Lookout
Henry Stewart
William Stone
John W. Tabler of Hyattstown
William N. Taylor, POW Ft. McHenry
Charles Byron Thomas
Edmund Thomas
Frank Thomas
Samuel Franklin Thomas
George Triplett, POW Pt. Lookout
Joseph H. Trundle of near Dickerson
Philip Van Bussum
Elijah Veirs of Poolesville, POW Old Capitol Prison
Frank Veirs of Poolesville
H. William Veirs of Poolesville
William Seneca Veirs of Poolesville, POW Pt. Lookout
Joseph Vinson of Poolesville
William H. Waesche of Edwards Ferry
Henry Waring, Philip Watts
Edward Welch, KIA Brandy Station
Henry Whelen
G. H. White, MIA Brandy Station
George Walter White of Poolesville
John Collinson White of Poolesville, POW Pt. Lookout
Samuel Chiswell White of Poolesville
Thomas Henry White of Poolesville, POW Old Capitol Prison
William C. White of Poolesville
Francis Thomas Williams of Poolesville

John O. Wise, POW Ft. McHenry
Zadock A. Yingling
        White's men served as guards to Ewell's division as they crossed the Potomac at White's Ford into Maryland without the wounded General Ewell. Upon their arrival in Poolesville they were greeted with cheers and a large crowd. White's men proceeded to Frederick and then returned to Virginia crossing at his farm where he found a Union battalion of infantry and cavalry. The infantry was captured and taken to Leesburg. His men then met the 2nd New York Cavalry and during the skirmish Captain White was shot in the throat.

        On September 4, 1862 J. E. B. Stuart's cavalry crossed the Potomac at White's Ford just south of where the Potomac Electric Power Company is presently located. The regimental bands played "Maryland, My Maryland" as the troops entered Montgomery County. Local citizens barricaded Union soldiers from leaving Poolesville, holding them at gunpoint until the Confederate forces arrived. The Union troops moved toward Washington City and took up positions to protect the Capitol. Colonel T. T. Munford's men were left at Poolesville as part of a cavalry screen while the remainder of Stuart's men continued toward Frederick after the residents of Poolesville gave provisions to the Southern forces.

        On September 8, 1862 Munford's forces of Virginia's 2nd, 7th, and 12th Mounted Cavalry troops were attacked just east of town by the 8th Illinois and 3rd Indiana Cavalry Regiments under General John F. Farnsworth. The women of Poolesville took refuge in their basements as the firing began, which sent rounds right over the rooftops. Munford's men moved from east of Poolesville to the road to Barnesville where they took a stand. After about thirty minutes the Confederates fled to the neighboring town of Barnesville where they met Munford's men again the following day. Munford's forces departed for Frederick to meet up with Stuart before going on to South Mountain and Antietam. Back in Poolesville Major General Darius Couch led his Division of the 4th Corps through town on September 10, 1862 en route to the same battlefields by way of Barnesville.

        Dr. Edward E. Stonestreet was the Examining Surgeon recruited to bolster the Union forces from Medley District. He examined 335 men between September 11 and October 18, 1862 and listed them as exempted, drafted or whether they had purchased a substitute. Some of the medical reasons listed for exemption are revealing. Extracted from his list are men in the vicinity of Poolesville who were drafted:

George W. Butler	Thomas Phillips
Charles M. Butler, Jr.	Thomas Piles
James B. Elgin	William H. Pleasants
Abe T. N. Eversol	David S. Pleasants
William C. Houghes	James W. Reid
George W. McIntosh	Charles R. Regan
James Miller	William Rallison

John W. Mossburg   Charles Smith
Henry Josiah Norris   James Trundle
Thomas Oxley   Ayres Veirs
    Some of these men crossed the Potomac River and joined the Rebs, others served in the Union Army. The following men paid for substitutes: merchant Thomas R. Hall - James Belcher of Boston, farmer Richard H. Lowe - John Wagner of Baltimore, farmer William Metzger, Jr. - Milton Armstrong of Philadelphia, farmer Thomas W. Vinson - James Perry of Rhode Island, and farmer John Henry Williams - Aron Andberry of New York.
    The following men were exempted: farmer Gary Aud, blacksmith Richard Beeding, carpenter Bartholomew Beall, farmers George Brewer and James Henry Beall, laborer Thomas H. Butcher, blacksmith James L. Beall, farmer David T. Cissell, saddler Edwin Cruit, farmers Thomas D. Darby, John H. Dade and Alexander Dade, wheelwright Archibald P. Eversall, Justice of the Peace John R. Fletchall, farmers Isaac Fyffe, Thomas Fyffe, Jr., Thomas N. Gott, and George H. Hughes, John R. Hoskins, farmer Robert Hillard, carpenter Thomas H. Money, farm laborer Peter N. Mossburg, carpenters James Ingalls and Nathan E. Miles, blacksmith George D. Powell, farmers Thomas Poole, William Wallace Poole, and Robert Smoot, photographer Benjamin F. Reid, farmers Perry L. Trundle, Henry O. Talbott, Napoleon B. Vinson, and Washington W. Vinson, lawyer Cumberland R. Veirs, farmers Benjamin R. White, Daniel T. White, and William N. Young.
    The following men were examined and not categorized:

Robert H. Aud	Frank H. Vinson	James L. Norris
Finton Aud	Robert P. Vinson	James R. Miles
Joseph Aud	Joshua A. Vinson	George C. Fisher
John B. Byrd	William F. Veirs	John R. Hall
John T. H. Carey	Charles Vinson	Cincinnatus Hall
William Chiswell	Charles Smith	Benjamin Cator
George Johnson	James Lowe	William H. Jones
William Jones	Howard Griffith	Thomas Johnson
John Jones, Jr.	John W. Hillard	George E. Keyser
James S. Padgett	Benjamin White	James Merchant
Joseph B. Piles	Joseph White	James W. Morrison
John W. Poole	Frederick C. Young	Thomas McDonough
James F. Poole	Henry Young	Jackson Moulden
Thomas H. Poole	Isaac Young	William Nokes
Benson Talbott	Robert T. Cooley	John Padgett
George W. Spates	William H. Cooley	Richard Stallings
William T. Vinson	Thomas Cator	Richard F. Trail
William T. Walter		

In the fall of 1862 Poolesville was held by General Samuel P. Heintzelman. His 3rd Corps occupied the town while General Lee was located in Shepardstown and the Federal Army of the Potomac's main column was across the Potomac from Harper's Ferry. Heintzelman received intelligence from the Sugarloaf Mountain signal station that General J. E. B. Stuart's men had broken from the main column and were heading west from Hyattstown. Early in the morning of October 12, 1862 the Federal Third Corps began a march intending to engage Stuart's men in battle. However, one of Stuart's men was a native of the area and knew of an old farm lane, changing their approach to the Potomac River. Captain Benjamin Stephen White guided them toward the Mouth of Monocacy where the two rivers meet. Stuart's men skirmished with Alfred Pleasonton's guards, pushing them aside. Stuart's men crossed at White's Ford before Gen. Heintzelman's main forces arrived. Stuart had split his column on this push toward the river, and the artillery unit was engaged briefly by the 99th Pennsylvania Infantry. Deployed along the rim of the nearby rock quarry and commanded by Colonel E. R. Biles, they were bluffed by the true size of the column who began firing cannon rounds. The 99th withdrew and the guns were pontooned across the river and set into position to cover the crossing of the troops.

During Captain White's recuperation the men were officially organized into a battalion on October 28, 1862. The men were mustered in by Colonel Bradley T. Johnson. Five companies were incorporated at this time, with an additional sixth company added later. The original group became Company A with Captain Frank Myers, and lieutenants William F. Barrett, Richard Marlow, and Ben Conrad. Company B was "Chiswell's Exiles" with Captain George Walter Chiswell, Joshua R. Crown, adjutant and 1st lieutenant; and Edward Chiswell and Nicholas Dorsey as 2nd lieutenants. White was promoted to Major and returned to active duty in mid-November.

In early November of 1862 the Third Corps withdrew from Poolesville, leaving only a small garrison of thirty men. At dawn on November 25, Captain Chiswell led Company B's charge of Poolesville. They captured sixteen Union soldiers of the 11th New York Cavalry guarding supplies, two telegraph operators, their equipment, medical supplies, and raided the local stores. Chiswell gave the local men a few hours at home and then they returned to camp, paroling the prisoners after destroying their supplies.

On November 29 Major White was wounded in the thigh during an attack not far from his Loudoun County farm. Dr. Edward Wootton was en route to join the battalion when he was captured and taken to Leesburg. White's wound was superficial and he remained in command.

On December 14, 1862 the Union troops in Poolesville numbered only forty men. Elijah White, now a major, led 63 men to the Presbyterian Church where the Baptist services were being held, as they had not yet built their own church. White's men surrounded the building while the 11th New York Cavalry was attending services conducted by Reverend Samuel White. As the men attempted to escape, a sergeant was killed and the others soldiers were captured. Union soldiers who were quartered in the old Town Hall began firing on the Rebels and in the resulting skirmish two Union soldiers were killed and eight wounded. Realizing they were outnumbered, the Union troops surrendered. Confederate Samuel Jenkins was killed by friendly fire. The raiders spent a few hours in Poolesville before returning to White's farm. They brought back over 40 horses, arms, clothing, food, and wagons. The 21 captives were marched to White's Ferry where they were pardoned as prisoners of war, released, and allowed to walk back to Poolesville. On December 29, 1862 the Montgomery County Sentinel reported that Thomas R. Hall's General Store had been completely stripped of all stock during the raid.

Following the Confederate raid, the Union Army was reinforced by Colonel Albert Jewett's Brigade in January of 1863. The brigade included the 10th Massachusetts artillery and 6th Michigan Cavalry and was known as the "Corps of Observation." Four infantry regiments were also sent: 23rd Maine, 10th Vermont, 14th New Hampshire and 36th Massachusetts were sent to Poolesville. In the spring materials for a pontoon bridge were sent to lock 25 [Edward's Ferry] on the Chesapeake and Ohio Canal. The engineers had the bridge constructed across the Potomac River in a matter of hours. Many men crossed this bridge and continued up the towpath of the canal toward the Mouth of Monocacy.

Union Forces on Main Street, Winter 1862

The women back home often sang the songs of the unit. "Chiswell's Exile Band" by John Crown was also sung by the men of Co. B and after the war at gatherings on Memorial Day and other occasions. "The Old Virginia Thirty-fifth" was another song sung by loved ones hoping their men would return.

Elijah V. White was promoted to Lieutenant Colonel on February 4, 1863. The men spent several months near New Market, Virginia, drilling and planning for next campaign. General Wade Hampton led the 35th Battalion through western Virginia, taking part in General Jones' raid and the battle of Brandy Station. One casualty on May 22, 1863 was Wallace Sellman of Company B. On June 9 nearly 100 men of the 35th Battalion were killed. Among the seriously wounded was Captain George Walter Chiswell. Another Captain was captured and remained a prisoner of war for the duration of the conflict.

After surprising a supply train and destroying the tracks near Point of Rocks, White's men joined General John B. Gordon's Brigade on their way to the Susquehanna River via Emmitsburg on the 25th of June. General Robert E. Lee, and Major General John F. Reynolds were in Poolesville that day. Major General Winfield Scott Hancock and Brigadier General Alfred Pleasonton arrived the following day with the Union Cavalry Corps followed by Major General Joseph Hooker who made his headquarters in Poolesville on June 27 and 28.

The men of Co. B 35th Virginia Cavalry were the first Confederate forces on the scene, Friday June 26, 1863. They chased the Adams County Cavalry from their positions and then scouted the town of Gettysburg. The first casualty of the campaign was George Washington Sandoe, killed by a Confederate of the 35th Virginia Cavalry while on patrol in the town, ironically they were also the last regiment to leave the battlefield.

On Saturday June 27, 1863 Colonel White led his men to Hanover with orders to destroy telegraph lines and railroad bridges. On their return trip, July 1, they found a few horses and provisions. During the battle the men of Poolesville guarded General Gordon's flank, scouted for Union troops that might attack from the sides or rear, and buried the dead. Eight of the men, including John Moiner and Edward Simpson of Co. B, were captured, but none were wounded or killed. On July 5 they were the rear guard for Gordon's troops, and stopped in Hagerstown on the 7th, crossing the Potomac River into Virginia a week later.

On August 27 one hundred of Colonel Elijah V. White's men crossed the Potomac River again. Their surprise attack on the 11th New York Cavalry [Scott's 900] was highly praised by General J. E. B. Stuart. With only one wounded, they took sixteen prisoners and thirty-five horses. The Confederate forces also raided the stores of Jesse T. Higgins, Fletchall, Heffner and William T. Walter. The Poolesville Presbyterian Church was used as a hospital during this period.

On November 29, 1863, Colonel White's men on order from General Thomas Rosser charged the Union Cavalry while yelling at the top of their lungs.

Rosser's reference to the men as "Comanches" became the nickname of White's Battalion from that point on. Back in Poolesville the 8th Illinois Cavalry enforced martial law during the winter of 1863-64. In March the 11th New York was sent to Louisiana and the 2nd Massachusetts Cavalry replaced them in Poolesville.

Following the Battle of the Monocacy in 1864 General Jubal Early attempted to capture Washington. Creating a diversion, Colonel John Mosby's men skirmished with the 6th Ohio Cavalry while Early attacked Fort Stevens. Early passed through Poolesville on July 14 headed for the Potomac River with the VI Corps of Major General Horatio G. Wright giving chase through Poolesville.

The last regiment to hold Poolesville was the 16th New York Cavalry. They were withdrawn in the Spring of 1865. As the final skirmishes ended between Lynchburg and Appomattox men on horseback were able to ride northeast without capture. A few teamsters driving supply wagons could not make the fast break, and were present to take the oath on April 9, 1865. The men of Company B were: David G. Carlisle, Private Lewis A. Eader, Private James M. Matthews, Private William Oden, and Private Philip Van Bussum.

Most men of the 35th Battalion never attended the ceremonious surrender at Appomattox Court House, but instead turned their horses toward home and rode from Lynchburg with fewer men then had initially been in a company. They disbanded on April 10, 1865 after a speech by Lieutenant Colonel White at Madison Heights, Virginia. The Montgomery County men rode to a parole office near Edward's Ferry and received the necessary papers to avoid capture. Colonel White was paroled at Winchester on April 24, 1865. He was later elected sheriff, ran a granary with Dr. Edward Wootton at the C & O Canal, and operated White's Ferry. He was also president of the People's National Bank of Leesburg.

A tablet was erected by the Ladies Auxiliary of Monocacy in memory of the local men who fought for the Confederate States of America. In Monocacy Cemetery of Beallsville the following names are listed: Wallace Sellman, Samuel Collinson White, Alonzo Sellman, Captain George Walter Chiswell, George W. Butler, Major Benjamin Stephen White, Elias Moulden, John P. Bouic, Francis E. Burch, Elijah Veirs, Henry B. Veirs, Elias Price, James W. Reed, Lieutenant Edward Jones Chiswell, Francis T. Williams, William Franklin Dade, William Seneca Veirs, Benjamin John Jones, John Collinson White, Richard S. Stallings, Richard Poole Hays, William Harrison Dickerson, William H. Waesche, Charles Martin Butler, John William Holland, Thomas H. White, John B. Munger, Michael Thomas Pyles, and B. Franklin Pyles.

Poolesville began repairing the vast amount of damage left by both armies and returned to a quiet town. The schoolhouse received reparation funds from the Federal Government. The stores began restocking merchandise and the town had its own brass band. Incorporated in 1867, Poolesville is the second oldest incorporated municipality in Montgomery County. The town is six miles from White's Ferry, the last existing ferry to cross the Potomac River. During the post-war years of industrialization, the local economy changed from small farms to commercial agriculture. Larger towns offered a larger variety of products and services than Poolesville did, and as roads improved, some customers went elsewhere, leaving the historic character of the town unaltered for many years.

Remembering the men of White's Virginia 35th Battalion the Lime Kiln Bard penned the following lines:

Bugler, sound boots and saddles,
Call the Comanches once again,
Wake them from their peaceful slumber,
Where so many long have lain.

Call the intrepid daring leader,
Tell him that the foe is near,
A little louder sound your bugle
Why it is they do not hear?

Where is the 35th Battalion,
Can it be they left the field?
Always first in every conflict
Always the very last to yield.

Men with nerve, men with mettle,
men whose hearts knew not fear,
Men who fought for home and fireside
And the land the loved most dear.

Bugler, sound boots and saddles
They answer not? Well, let them rest
Their warfare over, they are sleeping
And perhaps 'tis for the best.

Yes the bold and daring troopers
Here laid their swords away to rust,
Many with their gallant leader
Now have gone "From dust to dust."

But their country has not forgot them
In our hearts they ever live
And in their memory these verses
I most freely give.

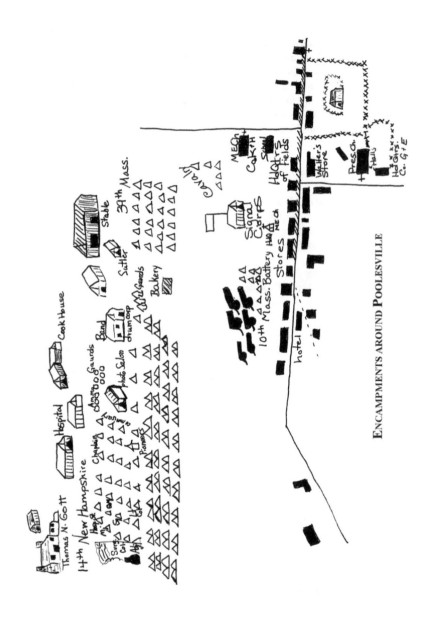

ENCAMPMENTS AROUND POOLESVILLE

24

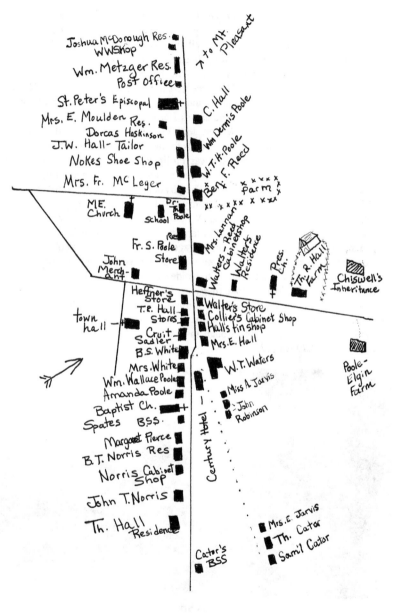

1865 Town Map

25

An 1870 business list reflects the growth of the area. Nathan S. White, Sr. was a fire insurance agent. George W. McIntosh was still the tinsmith. Shoemakers included John Grimes, William Nokes, and Charles S. Grimes. Benjamin F. Reed was still painting houses. The millers were William and Charles Mansfield and Thomas Milford. Wheelwrights were Jacob Bodmer, John W. Norris and Henry J. Norris. The carpenters of the day were Charles W. Norris, James H. Money, John O. Merchant, and Joseph Cator. The blacksmiths were Samuel Cator, Archey Brander, and James Hardy. The village merchants were William N. Hays, William T. Walter, John G. Poole, and Mary Ella Florence Matthews. She made hats and fancy goods for her millinery shop. The tailor was John W. Hall and the cabinetmaker was Philip Reed, Jr. Edwin Cruit had an apprentice saddle and harnessmaker named Seymour Connell, and Joshua Davis had a saddle shop on another street. The physicians were Dr. Edward Wootton and Dr. Nathan S. White, Jr. The Century Hotel was run by James U. Miles and the tavern was run by Hilleary Pyles. William C. Hoskinson was employed as a clerk in a store. Many still engaged in farming in the vicinity such as: Christian Heffner, John T. Fletchall, William Metzger, Frederick Sprigg Poole, John H. Nolens, and Thomas H. Poole. Those who had retired from a trade or farming found Poolesville an attractive place to reside such as William Poole, Barnard T. Norris, Samuel C. Young, Richard Pyles, Philip Reed, and Margaret Pearce. Others were farm laborers, teachers, ministers or handymen. Samuel Boling Milford recalled horse races held on Main Street on Saturdays during this time period. The horses ran right through town after the bets were all placed. The population in 1879 was 275.

Main Street

26

Chapter Three
Recent History

"But days that tried the souls of men
were banished by the angels of peace,
and Poolesville rose from doubt and dismay
while happiness wore a new lease." — John Will Hall

During the winter of 1898-99 Poolesville received heavy accumulations of snow. Notice the hotel in the center where the Town Hall stands today and the height of the snow piles from clearing paths in which to walk.

When automobiles arrived in Poolesville so did gasoline pumps. In the photograph above a Texaco pump stands in front of Merchant's Hotel. Before electric pumps, the fuel was pumped into the holding tank at the top and then drained down into the tank under the hood.

In the early days of baseball, games and practices were held at the "Baseball Grounds" which appear on the 1879 map. At that time they were near the present intersection of Fisher Avenue and Norris Road. The 1905 team is pictured below. The '05 team's back row: Luther Cruit, Dawson Trundle, Bridge Spates, Charles Sellman; middle: Ernest Beall, Jess Mossburg, Maynard Sellman, Hartle Wootton, Grover Pyles; front: Harry Talbott, Randolph Luhn. The 1918 team is pictured on the following page, top photograph.

POOLESVILLE BASEBALL TEAM 1905

POOLESVILLE BASEBALL TEAM MEMBERS 1918

POOLESVILLE BAND MEMBERS

During the 1910's-1930's the Poolesville Band rehearsed at the Town Hall. Led by Walter K. Matthews, there were approximately 15-20 members. They performed in uniforms for the Hyattstown carnival, The Upper Montgomery County Volunteer Fire Department carnival in Beallsville, and Church picnics at Forest Grove, Lovettsville and Stumptown. In later years the band rehearsed in the basement of Charles Rozier Bodmer's home east of Poolesville. After about 1970 the band was discontinued. The lower photograph on the preceding page shows the Matthews family: Doris, Vivian, Hubert, Walter, and Walter K. Matthews, Sr. The photograph below has George Holland, Roy Swank, Charles Knill, Earl Stottlemyer, Doris Matthews, W. S. Swank, Harold Thompson, Edith Thompson, Frank Knill, Vivian Matthews, Charles Orme, Walter Matthews, Charles Rozier Bodmer, Hubert Matthews, Harold Smoot, and Walter K. Matthews, Sr.

The Poolesville Telephone Company was formed in 1909 by Byron W. Walling, Howard W. Spurrier, A. Dawson Trundle, Albert Wootton, William T. Griffith, Clagett C. Hilton, Thomas O. White, William H. Chambers, David R. Hershey and Reginald Darby. Harry Willard was in charge of the equipment and maintenance. The first telephone in Poolesville is pictured below. The first switchboard was located in Emma Hodgson's house and later in the house on Fisher Avenue pictured on the following page. In 1921 the C & P Telephone Company was built. It was located on Elgin Avenue and is pictured on the following page in the lower photograph. It has been converted into a residence.

POOLESVILLE'S FIRST TELEPHONE

TELEPHONE LOCATIONS

33

In 1912 the Poolesville Women's Club was organized with Mrs. Thomas Hall as president. In 1921 Fisher Avenue was paved. When the streets were named, Fisher Avenue was chosen for Main Street in honor Carl Fisher. The road to Beallsville was renamed in honor of the Elgin Family. Beall Circle was named for Scott Beall, local builder. Back Street was renamed Wootton Avenue in honor of Dr. Wootton. Norris Road was named for the Norris Family who had run the livery stable in Poolesville.

A fire destroyed the business district of the town on August 16, 1923. The fire started in Thomas Hoskinson's store and Dora Hall sounded the alarm. Despite efforts to contain the blaze seven businesses were destroyed. The Hoskinson's General Merchandise store lost $6,000 worth of stock and the $3,000 building. The Ice Cream and Lemonade Shop operated by Carl Fisher lost $2,500 worth of stock and the $1,500 building. The post office lost $300 in fixtures and the $5,200 building. Howard Spurrier's clothing, furniture and shoe store lost $17,500 in stock and the $7,500 building. Albert Wootton's store lost $1,000 in merchandise and the $12,500 building. The tinsmith shop of Charles Morrison lost $1,500 in stock and the $2,500 building. The residence of Mrs. Charles Morrison lost $500 in furniture and the $2,500 home. Also damaged in the fire were the Soper Barber Shop, Zachariah M. Compher's, Dr. Edwin Pyles Drug Store, Jacob Bodmer's Shoe Shop, Hall's Tailor Shop, Elgin Brother's store, and the homes of Harry Kohlhoss, Thomas N. Gott House, and the residence of Dora and Rebecca Hall. Rev. Berkley Griffith, rector of the Episcopal Church, rushed in to the post office and saved the bags of mail, dragging them into the street. On the following page are two photographs of the fire and the aftermath.

Poolsville, Md. During the fire, Main St., Aug. '23.

1923 Fire

After the Fire

Other serious fires destroyed property in 1931 and February 6, 1953. On December 17, 1940 the Monocacy Lions Club held their first meeting. Meetings were held in various locations including Barnesville Town Hall from 1947-1953 and the home of Spencer Fisher. After spearheading the concept and funding for the Upper Montgomery Volunteer Fire Department the meetings were held there after 1953. Comus Inn was the meeting spot for a few years, then in the 1970's the club has met at the Meadowlark Inn, but currently they meet at the Poolesville Baptist Church. The charter members were: Benoni D. Allnutt, A. Leland Clark, Charles H. Davis, Edward J. Dunphy, Charles W. Elgin, John E. Elgin, Carl T. Fisher, Charles W. Fritz, Mason W. Gray, Rev. Carl J. Hess, William B. Hilton, John R. Hunter, Charles H. Jamison, Lloyd J. Jones, Ernest R. Lillard, Charles Elmer Orme, Bruce P. Phillips, Harry C. Rhodes, C. William Roberts, C. Kyle Ruble, Charles G. Sellman, Richard B. Sellman, Byron W. Thompson and C. Merrick Wilson. Presidents of the Lions Club: 1940 C. Merrick Wilson, 1941 Lloyd J. Jones, 1942, Charles H. Davis, 1943 Harry C. Rhodes, 1944 Charles H. Jamison, 1945 Charles W. Elgin, 1946 A. Leland Clark, 1947 Charles Griffith, 1948 Rodger W. Williams, Jr., 1949 Benoni D. Allnutt, 1950 Lowell Moon, 1951 Maurice C. Ward, 1952 William B. Griffith, 1953 Humbert S. Kahle, 1954 George Welker, 1955 Lewis S. Rudasill, 1956 R. Edwin Brown, 1957 John Rolfe and William Frank, 1958 Edwin R. Johnson, 1959 Clifton O. Martin, 1960 John R. Spates, 1961 William D. Pyles, 1962 Charles E. Knill, 1963 A. Dawson Wootton, 1964 D. J. Willard, Jr., 1965 Richard Poole Brown, 1966 William P. Anderson, 1967 Paul Kelley, 1968 James Maurice Carlisle, 1969 John W. Davis, III, 1970 Thompson H. Butz, 1971 William C. Hilton, 1972 Audrey J. Shawver, 1973 C. Douglas Boyer, 1974 Edward Bacon, 1975 Roscoe H. Goeke, 1976 Dale Nestor, 1977 Rex Sturm, 1978 Earl Shreve, 1979 Daniel Yates, 1980 Herbert Brown, 1981 Bruce Wooden, 1982 Walter Prichard, 1983 Owen Laug, 1984 Richard Walden, 1985 Thomas James, 1986 Murray Deutchman, 1987 James Cangiano, 1988 Roy Selby, Jr. 1989 John Christie, 1990 William Nicholson Price, 1991 Charles Smallwood, III, 1992 Paul Stevens, 1993 Jonathan Chisholm, 1994 Joseph Ryba, 1995 Gary Burdette, 1996 Earl Shreve, 1997 Michael Wutherland, 1998 Peter Gallo, and 1999 Frank Austin.

In 1949 the Bethesda-Chevy Chase Chapter of the Izaak Walton League purchased the 366 acre J. DeWalt Willard farm off West Willard Road. The club was organized by 15 men in 1935. The house was destroyed by an arsonist in 1988 and was replaced in 1990. The facilities include trap and skeet fields, rifle and pistol range, archery ranges, and two fishing ponds. The chapter sponsors Cub Scout, Boy Scout and Girl Scout camping.

Poolesville resident Margaret W. Gray was the first woman foreman of a jury in a Maryland Courtroom in March of 1954. Poolesville observed their Sesqui-Centennial in 1954 with a celebration sponsored by the Board of Trade. Annual Poolesville Days continue to educate citizens and visitors about the heritage of the community. The population of Poolesville in 1960 represented the population increase in the United States every 54.6 minutes. The 298 citizens of Poolesville were photographed in front of the bank for a National Geographic article about the census. On October 7, 1961 a historical marker outlining Civil War events was unveiled by the Montgomery County Historical Society.

The town added a sewer system in 1965 and construction of the water system began in 1970. By 1974 Poolesville measured roughly two thousand acres. Town elections for commissioners are held every two years in November. Zoning ordinances began in 1957, and a Master Plan for the Town's development was adopted in 1964. In 1959 a new elementary school campus was opened. Just before the Christmas break kindergarten classes as well as first grade, second grade and one third grade class moved into the new facility. In 1962 the other third grade class moved from the High School campus. An addition which opened in September of 1963 housed the fourth, fifth and sixth grade classes, as well as the music room, library, science rooms, and cafeteria. The faculty numbered 16 that year including speech, art, physical education teachers and a librarian.

Civic groups and and other associations in Poolesville include the Elijah Veirs White Chapter of the Daughter's of the Confederacy which formerly met in the chapel at the Monocacy Cemetery and whose membership consisted of many Poolesville ladies, The Homemaker's Club, the Girls Scouts, and the Boy Scout's of America.

Western Upper Montgomery County Help or WUMCO was first known as Poolesville Help. The organization grew out of a need to provide medical assistance in the form of transportation and other help to local citizens. A food pantry began in the home of the late Beulah Harper and Jane Stearns provided transportation and other services. In 1968 WUMCO Help was founded by the Poolesville Community Relations Council and contributions came from local churches. In 1985 the organization was chartered by the State of Maryland as a non-profit corporation. Currently WUMCO Help receives monetary donations and volunteer support. The organization assists citizens with food, Holiday baskets, medicines, transportation, child care expenses, utilities and other needs.

The present Baptist Church started as a mission in 1971. The members met in the elementary school until 1975 when they purchased and remodeled the Chiswell house. In 1978 they broke ground for the present church and have since added space for classes. Pastors who have served this congregation include: Hector Huerta, Rev. Wry, Rev. Gates, Rev. Harris, Gene Thieman, Rev. Lafon Campbell, Rev. Jack Reynolds and Rev. L. M. Becknell.

The Poolesville Professional Center was built in 1977. In it is the first elevator in town. Some of the businesses over the years which were located here were: The First National Bank, Healthworks Fitness Center, dry cleaners, Images Hair Design, Dr. Valegra and Dr. Pike's Dentist Office, Poolesville Family Practice, and Dr. Footer, the foot doctor. Corporate Network Services, Inc. are there currently. Poolesville Plaza presently includes The First National Bank, Discount Tire and Auto Service, Images Hair Design, a day care center, and Selby's IGA store. The Poolesville Town Center houses Frederick County National Bank, Poolesville Veterinary Clinic Tack Shop, Poolesville library and Oriental Gourmet. Magruder Plaza houses Colonial Opticians, Dr. Leonard Sax, Beer and Wine Store, CVS, Dr. David Morra, D. D. S., and Little Caesars' Pizza. The Western County Pool was built in 1990 and is home to the Poolesville Swim Team. The population of Poolesville in 1995 was 4,200. The present Chamber of Commerce Officers are Linda Lewis, Lisa Selby, Dennis Prescott, Karen Williams and Maggie Nightingale. The Board of Directors consists of Malcolm Brown, Neal Brown, Jon Chisholm, Nancy Fost, Frank Jamison, Eddie Kuhlman, Billy Poole, and Maria Veillette.

"Our Lady of the Presentation" Roman Catholic Church is currently under construction on Fisher Avenue. Currently Rev. Y. David Brault celebrates mass at the Poolesville Elementary School. The rectory is located behind the church site.

Poolesville is governed by a group of five commissioners. The officials are elected to a four-year term and are unpaid. They elect a president, or mayor; and a vice-president. The commissioners meet twice a month at St. Peter's Hosler Hall and are responsible for policies, zoning, and planning. Other positions include town clerk, town manager, and various employees assisting with road maintenance, landscaping, parks, and administration.

The mayors of Poolesville have been: Joseph M. White, Howard Spurrier, Stanley Umstead, Gorman L. Butler, Bill R. Bliss, Gerald Morningstar, Eugene Halmos, Jr., Steven Ward, Samuel Zattiero, Charles W. Elgin, Sr., Darryl M. Kuka, Roy E. Johnson, and Andrew W. Johnson.

On August 21, 1819 the name Poolesville was officially listed with the Post Office Department.

Postmasters

Dennis Lackland	10 Dec 1810	John Poole's Store
Joseph Poole	27 Jul 1829	Benjamin & Joseph Poole's Store
Richard Poole	25 Feb 1831	
Hillary W. Darnell	3 Jan 1832	
Fielder Darnell	17 Mar 1838	
Frederick Sprigg Poole	7 Sep 1839	Poole's Store
Alexander E. Soper	15 May 1854	
Philip Reed	23 Jun 1855	Reed's Cabinet Shop
William Metzger	20 Jul 1861	Metzger's near St. Peter's
Samuel Cator	4 Aug 1869	Cator's Blacksmith Shop
Thomas Hoskinson	27 Jun 1877	
Samuel Cator	30 Jun 1877	Cator's Blacksmith Shop
John T. Norris	13 Aug 1885	Norris' Store
John H. Allnutt	12 Jul 1889	
Arthur Poole Fletchall	13 Feb 1894	
John H. Allnutt	4 Apr 1898	
Silas Y. Browning	23 Jul 1900	
Harry L. Willard	15 May 1908	Wootton & Elgin's Store
Arthur P. Fletchall	4 May 1914	Charles Norris' House
Ernest G. Willard	24 May 1922	Norris' & later the Willard Building
Charles W. Elgin	1 Aug 1940	Elgin's Store-Cruit's Shop
Ronald Foster	31 Dec 1973	New Postal Facility
Janice Stottlemyer	18 Oct 1980	Poolesville Post Office

Rural Free Delivery service at Poolesville was established on February 1, 1904. Jacob Bodmer was the first carrier, and his son Charles R. Bodmer, World War I Veteran, was the second carrier. The new Postal Facility opened in April 1976.

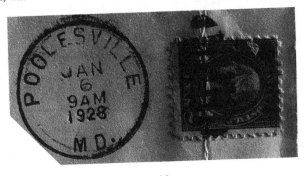

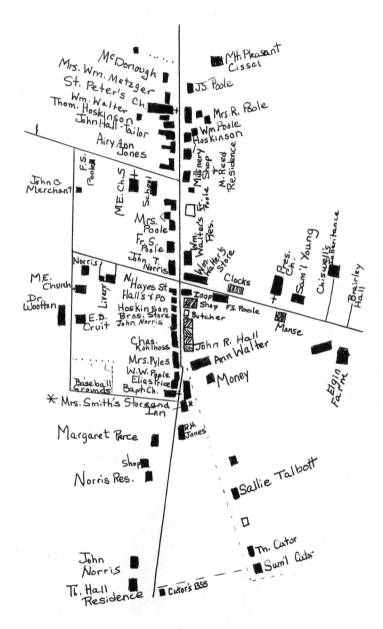

1879 Town Map

40

Lewis Reed, Blacksmith
William Norris, Carpenter
Dr. T. H. Schaeffer, Dentist
William N. Hays, Merchant
Charles Kohlhoss, Merchant
Thomas Milford, Miller
Dr. Ayler, Physician
Dr. Edward Wootton, Physician
Elias Price, Shoemaker

E. Hall, Carpenter
James H. Money, Carpenter
Thomas Randolph Hall, Merchant
Thomas & William Hoskinson, Merchants
John T. Norris, Merchant
M. Reed, Milliner
Dr. Walling, Physician
Charles Grimes, Shoemaker
W. T. H. Poole, Veterinary Surgeon

Straub and Son, Carriage Manufacturers

George Brewer
William Brewer
Humphrey Cissel
William Cissel
Edward Chiswell
George Chiswell
Edwin D. Cruit
John Dade
Frederick A. Dawson
George C. Fisher
Martin Fisher
John Fletchall
Isaac Fyffe
Thomas N. Gott
Howard Griffith
Aaron B. Hersberger
H. T. Hempstone
T. Hempstone
Robert T. Hilliard
Thomas Hoskinson
A. Hughes
William D. Hughes
Robert J. Isherwood
Miss Jones
Nathan Jones
Richard Henry Jones

William T. Jones
Richard Lowe
Charles Metzger
William Metzger
James Miles
Uriah Miles
Rose Anna Money
John T. Norris
Nathan Dickerson Poole
Frederick Sprigg Poole
John Sprigg Poole
Richard Poole
Thomas H. Poole
Wallace Poole
William Poole
Charles Price
Mrs. Pyles
William Schaffer
Charles Sellman
Mrs. Smith
Benson Talbott
Sallie Talbott
James Trundle
Ann Walter
William Walter
Frank White

Charles Willard
J. Willard
John H. Williams
David Young
Henry Young
Isaac Young
W. T. Young

CHAPTER FOUR
RESIDENCES AND BUILDINGS

1. Briarley Hall

This private school began as Briarley Hall Female Academy in 1874, founded by Mrs. Mary E. Porter and her daughter Williametta E. Porter. The Porter's purchased 12 acres of "Chiswell's Inheritance" from Robert and Isabella Darby Isherwood for the campus. The three story house with a front porch spanning the front of the building served as home and class rooms to the girls. The second and third floors had a central hallway with rooms on each side. Subjects included English, elocution, philosophy, chemistry, physiology, botany, French taught by Monsieur Blanchard, and art and music taught by Miss Willie. Another teacher during this era was Nettie Martin. Miss Willie contracted pneumonia and died at Briarley Hall on April 6, 1883. Mary Porter continued the school for a few years and then sold it to her nephew's wife Mary Gassaway in 1886. The school was renamed Briarley Hall Seminary and the house was enlarged. Classes such as English, history, literature, mathematics, vocal and instrumental music, drawing, painting and languages were taught by Florence and Laura Gassaway, Jennie Birdsall, and Frances Bell. Mary Jane Pyles and Florence Pyles were among the day students who drove to and from school in a buggy.

Tuition was $175 per year for boarding students and $25 for day students. Students enjoyed tennis and croquet on the wide lawn but never left the campus unattended. Those attending church services were chaperoned. Commencement exercises were held in Poolesville's Town Hall. After Mrs. Gassaway's death in 1905 the school continued for a year under her daughter's leadership. The following three years Mrs. Theodora Hooker managed the school adding a School of Finance, which she taught personally. Below: students and teachers in 1897. Front row: Lizzie Clarke, Sallie Williams, Mary Broome, Jessie MacDonald, Sadie Reading, Alice Wise. Second row: Sallie Griffith, Anna Darby, Emily Williams, Eleanor Moffatt, Hallie Norris, Nellie Pleaster, Edith Clark, Freddie Clagett, Miss Plaster [teacher]. Carrie Gott. Third row: Evelyn Orrison, Betty Williams, Florence Pyles, Birdee Rouzee, Eleanor Chiswell, Stella Hoskinson, Mary Hoskinson, Dawson Williams, Laura Clarke, Rachel Clark, Miss Florence Gassaway [teacher], Dolie Jones, Miss Jennie Young [teacher].

Pictured below are six young ladies who attended Briarley Hall c. 1904 front: Myrna Miles, ?, C. Beulah Nicholson, back: ?, Mabel Poole, Maude Getzendanner.

BRIARLEY HALL BARRACKS

44

In September 1912 Briarley Hall Military Academy opened. The insignia featured the school's initials BHMA with God, Country, Courtesy, Chivalry, Courage, Manliness, Honor and Obedience. Tuition for the year was $325 plus textbooks. One of the teachers was Elizabeth White Tipton. The house was renamed "The Barracks."

Gas lighting illuminated the rooms and steam radiators kept students warm in the winter. A split rail fence surrounded the campus which also included a ball field, dugout, and clubhouse. The superintendent, Captain Sidney Lodge, had his office on the first floor with a telephone and typewriter on his roll top desk and his diplomas on the wall. Also located on the ground floor were the library, reading room and dining room. Classrooms were on the second floor. Students had their own desks and each wore a cadet uniform. Captain Lodge taught English, history and military science; Captain Miller Cassedy taught languages and science and Captain Carroll Dolman taught mathematics. Charles W. Woodward was an instructor during this period, he later became a judge in Montgomery County. Dr. Elijah W. White was the Post Surgeon and Mrs. W. B. Magruder was the Matron. The study hall photograph below which was taken in 1916 shows 31 of the cadets.

Cadets also participated in a variety of clubs. Such clubs included dramatic club, track squad, baseball, Big B Football team and glee club. The glee club was accompanied by violins and a mandolin. The rehearsed in the school library located on the first floor. The dining room was also on the first floor. A peddlar man came regularly to sell items to students and faculty.

BIG 'B' FOOTBALL TEAM

Cadet Quarters were located on the third floor with single beds lined along the wall and windows in between. Desks and bureaus were placed wherever space allowed. Bathrooms and showers were added in 1912. Along with standard subjects, cadets learned to scale walls, shoot targets, parade with drum and bugle corps, raise and lower the flag, and to participate in an annual encampment with full military maneuvers, drills and discipline.

TRACK SQUAD

48

Pictured below, the 1915 baseball team captured the Montgomery County Baseball Championship by winning 16 of their 24 games. Some of the teams they beat were: Baltimore City College 12-0; FPS 42-0; Charlotte Hall 6-0; Stewart's College 8-5; Charlotte Hall 3-2; Business High School 3-1; Central High School 12-8. The BHMA graduates of 1917 were S. W. Tull, C. C. Clarke, H. R. Berger, Jr., S. P. Hersperger and H. C. Joyner. Briarley Hall closed in 1930 because families could no longer afford to pay tuition during the Depression. A termite infestation caused serious damage to the house and it was demolished c. 1940. Today a modern home is on the site of the barracks and the guard house, recreation building, and gates are the only markers of the school.

1915 BHMA Baseball team

49

1917 BHMA Baseball Team

Chiswell's Inheritance

2. Chiswell's Inheritance

Stephen Newton Chiswell patented "Joseph's Choice" with 90 acres upon the birth of his son Joseph in 1747. During Joseph's youth, Stephen Newton Chiswell added acreage to the property. Upon reaching the age of majority, Joseph inherited over 300 acres and called it "Chiswell's Inheritance." The Georgian style brick, five bay house was constructed in 1796. When Joseph and his wife Sarah Newton Chiswell moved in to the house, they had nine children and needed such a large house in which to raise them. Two more children were born here. The house has unusual woodwork and fret work, most notably over the library door, in the Chippendale pattern. The living room has cabinets set in the wall, flanked by doors and a carved mantle around the fireplace. The house had a separate kitchen which was later joined. The beehive oven which was used for baking collapsed, but the outline and it's access are still visible. The fireplace in the old kitchen still has it's crane for cooking pots to hang from. The central stairwell is three stories high, the attic is one and a half stories. The entire house was cut out and laid on the lawn. Numerals were drawn on each joint and reassembled as it was built with mortise and tenant construction. Joseph Chiswell deeded land to each of his children as they married, and hence at his death none needed to purchase the homeplace. Granddaughter Sarah Fletchall married William Matthews and they purchased the house in 1837. In 1845 William Matthews sold land to the county for Elgin Road to be laid out. Both Chiswells and Matthews served in local regiments and before leaving for active duty a large ball was held on the grounds. During the Civil War livestock and crops were taken by both sides. Needing cash after the war, Matthews sold one acre lots along what is now Elgin Road and on Route 107. The Trustees of the Baptist church purchased lot 2 in 1864, John O. Merchant purchased lot 5, Edward Hoskinson purchased lot 7 and William T. Walter purchased lot 8 in 1862. In 1866 Thomas Poole bought several other lots from William Matthews. John Adams purchased 100 acres of the farm and in 1866 the remaining 150 acres were sold to John R. Hall. Various owners sold the farm over the next 31 years. In 1897 Dr. Thomas E. Johnson purchased the property and added the East and West porches. Mrs. Mason [Beryl E.] Gray purchased the property in 1930 and re-named it Grayhaven Manor. She had central heating and plumbing installed and the tenant house built. She operated a successful dairy here for a number of years. After her son's marriage to Florence White, they lived in the tenant house. In 1956 George O. and Maryann Kephart purchased the house. They had a first floor bedroom converted into a modern kitchen, the East and West porches were removed, and the title "Chiswell's Inheritance" was restored. In the 1960's a vineyard was planted and the wine produced here was also called Chiswell's Inheritance. Headstones on the property from this time period have been noted after plowing, suggesting a family cemetery was located here.

HENRY DAVIS HOUSE

ELIJAH METHODIST'S MANSE

3. Elijah United Methodist Church

The first church on this site was called Elijah Rest Methodist Episcopal. The Trustees William Taylor, John Adams, Peter Davis, Bennett Lea and Alfred Dorsey bought the property for $150 from Edward Hoskinson. The first pastor was Elijah Aukward. In 1909 the construction of a new frame church was undertaken under the leadership of Reverend D. L. Washington. In 1923 additional land was purchased for the parsonage. Reverend B. F. Hall was the first to occupy the new house. In 1950 a fire destroyed the church and all of the historical records it housed. The members worshipped in the Jerusalem Baptist Church while the present cinder block building was under construction. The church was designed by Elmer Jones. The following Pastors have served this church: Elijah Aukward, Thomas Brooks, Singleton Hughes, Washington Murray, Charles Arnold, D. L. Washington, Samuel Cole, Percy Middleton, B F. Hall, George Dent, W. N. Hold, E. P. Moon, William Polk, W. E. Brooks, Joseph Jennings, McKinley Jordan, Clifton Aukward, D. S. Sloane, Lovel Parham, Harvey Custis, R. S. Lacy, Harrison T. Randolph, Mark Hathorne, Miriam H. Jackson, Jesse E. Mayes, Fritz Outlaw, Howard C. Talley, Frances Stewart and John Chaney, Jr.

4. Love and Charity Hall School

In 1865 a frame school, twenty by thirty-three feet, was constructed for the black students of the Poolesville area. Built on lot 7 of Chiswell's Inheritance, the lot was fourteen square perches. In 1868 Montgomery County sold the building for $1. The school was a two-story frame building on the southwest corner of the lot. It had a bell tower and three double hung windows down each side, with a chimney on the rear wall. The school was called Love and Charity Hall School. Since the county no longer owned the school, they did not maintain it or provide a teacher. In 1893 the county bought the school back and listed it as the Poolesville Colored School. In 1927 a new school was constructed for the black children in the community. The contract went to Mr. Pope and Mr. Barry, and four acres were purchased for six hundred dollars from Mr. Mossburg. The old school building was sold to the church in 1932, under Rev. Moon. The building was torn down because of the deteriorated condition. On September 13, 1949 the second school located in Jerusalem was closed and the students were transported to the school in Sellman. The location is now used for the Montgomery County Road and Equipment Depot and "the beauty spot."

5. site of Harry M. Williams house

This was one of the lots parceled off of "Chiswell's Inheritance" by William
Matthews. The original house burned down late 1920's, and Harry Williams
rebuilt it on the same foundation. In 1951 he sold it to Mr. and Mrs. Louis Jones.
In 1968 Dr. William Butterball purchased the house. The present owners are
Sarah and Michael Defnet.

6. Benjamin White House

This house was built for Dr. Samuel B. Milford in 1908. Dr. Milford was the son of the miller, whose house and mill are long gone. Mr. and Mrs. Benjamin White purchased the house the same year. Mr. White was a cashier in local bank for many years and lived to the age of 102. The Whites continued to live here until the death of Mr. White in 1976. Dean Gray Wroth, granddaughter of the Whites and her husband Edward "Ted" Wroth III live here presently.

7. Hodgson House

This house was built c. 1915 for Estelle F. Hodgson and her daughter Emma. The photo was taken in 1916. For many years they operated the Central Exchange Telephone Office at this location, which was owned by the Poolesville Telephone Company. Miss Emma Hodgson was the chief operator of the switchboard. When the company converted the service to the dial system Miss Hodgson had a separate facility built to house the equipment on her property. The Chesapeake and Potomac Telephone Company purchased the Poolesville Telephone Company in 1921. The current owner of the house is Mrs. Nancy Hopkinson. The C & P building, located next to this house, has been converted into a residence.

8. Dr. Elijah W. White House

Located on the former Hall farm, this house was built by Charles Sellman and Scott Beall for Dr. Samuel B. Milford in 1907. The house previously was accessed from Elgin Road down a lane, but is now on a road in a sub-division. It was sold to Dr. and Mrs. Elijah W. White in 1908. The one-story wrap-a-round porch adds to the charm of the home. Dr. White also had his office here. He was a country doctor who made house calls and delivered many babies during his years in practice. The Whites raised four children here: Elizabeth, Mary, Elijah Jr., and Florence Helen. The current owners of the house are Thomas and Gail Lee.

9. Julius Hall's tenant house

This property was purchased from William Matthews by John Hall in 1862. The property became part of the Hall farm and passed to Julius Hall. One of the early African-American families in Poolesville, George Johnson, lived in this tenant house. In the 1930's George Johnson along with nine other family members lived here. The house was torn down in the mid-1950's. The town of Poolesville purchased the property and well #5 was drilled here. This well furnishes some of the water for the residents of Poolesville.

10. Presbyterian Manse

This house was built for Thomas R. Hall in 1827. During the Civil War troops camped on the farm behind the house and officers used the house as their headquarters. It became the Presbyterian Manse after 1864. Pastors lived in this manse until 1967 when the church was vacated. In 1970 the manse was used for Sunday School classes until the new hall was built in back of the manse. The following page shows the yard on a Sunday morning, and below a later view of the manse.

11. Presbyterian Church

This church was built in 1848 by Franklin Viers on land which was purchased from Elijah and Elizabeth Thompson for twenty dollars. The congregation was organized on April 16, 1847. The two charter members were Mrs. Lyles and Robert Graff who was also the first elder. The founding pastor was Rev. Charles Howard Nourse, a teacher employed by the Peter family of Montevideo near Seneca. On September 6, 1849 Thomas and Evelina Poole deeded this portion of "Poole's Right" to William Metzger, Robert Graff and William Matthews, Trustees of the Poolesville Presbyterian Church. In 1860 when the Poolesville Baptist Church was founded they had no building in which to worship. They began holding evening services in the Presbyterian Church, held by Reverend Samuel White. On Sunday December 14, 1862 Captain Elijah V. White's Cavalry unit surrounded the church during the evening service of the Baptists and waited for the Union troops to emerge. Twenty-one men were captured and marched to Edward's Ferry where the hostages were pardoned and released, while the Rebs and 60 horses crossed the Potomac River. Rev. D. Moutzer of Darnestown was the Presbyterian preacher when this church was used as a hospital following a skirmish in August of 1863. At that time the Baptist services moved to the schoolhouse. The Presbyterian Church's low membership forced it to be closed in 1953 but in 1956 it reopened with five members. It has continued to grow since that time. There are memorial windows for Judge Alfred D. Noyes 1907-1998 and his wife Anna F. Noyes 1901-1986, and Hannah Virginia Metzger who died January 25, 1895. The Pastors of the church have been:

Charles Howard Nourse	1847-1857
H. R. Smith	1858-1860
C. H. Powell	1860-1860
David Moutzer	1861-1865
C. N. Campbell	1869-1881
C. S. Lingamfelter	1881-1890
F. W. Pitman	1892-1902
R. L. McNair	1902-1906
A. W. Shaw	1908-1909
Lewis R. Watson	1914-1922
O. Y. Davis	1926-1927
Henry K. Pasma	1927-1948
Howard C. Cobbs	1949-1953
Fred S. McCorkle	1957-1960
Duncan Naylor	1960-1961
Timothy Lee	1961-1966
Filbert L. Moore, Jr.	1965-1967
Tom L. Torosian	1976-1982

Frances G. Wolf	1982-1990
George E. Taylor	1992-1998
Jane E. Dasher	1999-

12. Mossburg-Seymour House

Built of logs on a log foundation this house is of similar construction and scale as the John Poole house. It was built c. 1804 for Mr. Powell the shoemaker who had his shoe shop next door. It may have next served as a two-room school house during the village's early days. Artifacts found in and around the house validate the local legend that the school was located here, and that a loft above the school housed the teacher. The school was later converted into a residence and occupied by a '"bootlegger" and still later a clockmaker. The 1865 map indicates that William Walter owned the property. Ott Palmer lived here and the house was later purchased by Dr. Byron W. Walling whose daughter Mrs. Katherine Thompson sold it to Mrs. Carrie Mossburg Dwyer in 1936. Mr. William Seymour, the grandson of Mrs. Carrie Dwyer inherited the house. Presently his widow, Vera Seymour, resides here.

13. site of Cruit's House and Harness Shop

By 1804 Aeneas and Henrietta Campbell had a log house on this site. He was a cabinetmaker and the first Justice of the Peace in Poolesville. In 1862 William Walter bought the property from William Matthews and operated a store here. In the early 1900's a frame house was built here for Mr. and Mrs. Luther R. Cruit. The fenced yard was dotted with maple trees. Mr. Cruit was a harness maker and had his shop behind the house, facing Elgin Road. In 1906 Billy Walter had a store on the corner and after Mr. Cruit died in 1942 the property was sold to Stanley Umstead who had the yard cleared and built a service station. The post office was located here in the early 1950's. After it was moved to a more suitable location the dwelling was occupied by Mr. and Mrs. Joseph Remsburg. Later Mr. Umstead had both the house and harness shop demolished. In 1967 the First National Bank occupied the building where the harness shop once stood. When the Bank moved to it's present location in 1977 Jon Chisholm opened a video store in the building. The present service station on the corner is operated by Charles Glass.

14. St. Peter's Rectory

The St. Peter's Rectory was built in 1880 by W. G. Vernon at a cost of $1,200. The two and a half-story 40 by 30 foot house has three bays with a center gable. The one-story front porch is trimmed with gingerbread work. Two central chimneys once provided heat for both floors. The house sits on three acres of ground with a garden and field in the back. The rectory was sold in the mid-1980's to Thomas and Elizabeth Evans.

15. Walling-Halmos House

This house was built in 1883 for Dr. Byron W. Walling and his wife Emily Wailes Poole Walling. The lot was deeded on September 24, 1883 from Frederick S. and Florence Poole to Dr. Walling. The house was later owned by Joseph and Gertrude Haller who lived there for a number of years. After their deaths it was sold to Mrs. Fred Imirie. It is presently owned by Eugene Halmos, Jr. a former mayor of Poolesville.

16. Thompson-Hillard House

This house was built for Sidney and Katherine Walling Thompson in 1918. The deep front porch features double gables, with a center gable completing the pattern between them on the house. The Thompsons had two sons, Judge Byron Walling Thompson and Sidney Thompson. Sidney Thompson, Sr., a banker, traveled to and from work in Middleburg, Virginia via White's Ferry daily. The one and a half story house is now the home of George and Kathryn Hillard.

17. Memorial United Methodist Church

In 1892 a church was built for the Methodist Episcopal Church South congregation. The land was donated by William Griffith and the building committee consisted of Captain J. T. Fletchall, W. C. Hoskinson, Thomas Hoskinson, Howard W. Spurrier, James F. Poole, Nelson Young, Benson Talbott, and the Rev. William E. Woolf. The church was on the Montgomery Circuit and was dedicated in September of 1893 by Bishop Granbery. In 1912 the congregation added new pews, stained glass windows and a pipe organ. The church burned in a 1916 fire, and immediate plans to rebuild resulted in the present building dedicated in 1917. In 1928 the educational annex was dedicated and in 1939 the United Methodist Church brought the two congregations of Methodists together. The name of the church was changed on July 11, 1941 to Memorial United Methodist Church of Poolesville. The new parish hall and Sunday School facility were built in 1997.
The Pastors serving this church:

William E. Woolf	1892
Homer Shielding	1894
G. W. Bogle	1895
J. H. Dulaney	1896
James Anderson	1897
W. M. Stevens, assistant	1897
M. H. Keen	1898
Henry P. Hamill	1899
D. L. Reid	1900
J. H. Davidson	1902
B. V. Switzer	1904-8
J. T. Williams	1912
Melvin Thomas Tabler	1916
C. K. Ray	1919
E. W. Aaron	1921
Jacob N. Mast	1923
W. W. McIntyre	1926
William D. King	1930
Arthur E. Owens	1933
Ernest T. Harrison	1934
Lewis S. Rudasill	1938
Charles W. Lanham	1941
Charles Austin Michael	1943
Raymus R. Hillard	1952
David Winfrey	1954
Franklin Mills	1956
James R. Morgan	1957

Hayden L. Sparks	1963
Weller Lewis	1977
Clifford Kelbaugh	1982
Robert Hottinger	1985
Lewis McDonald	1991

Memorial Windows

The following persons have memorial windows in the church: Jane Griffith Waters, John E. Grubb, John H. and Martha Spurrier, George W. Reddick, Rev. William B. Spurrier, Amanda M. E., Edward J. and Susie B. Zimmerman, Acshah D. Jones, William T. and Elizabeth R. Jones, Rev. James T. Williams, Mary W. Williams, John T. and Mary Poole, G. Walter Fletchall, Elizabeth D. Griffith, William T. Griffith, Elizabeth Dade, Dorcas A. Hoskinson, James Edgar Grubb, Emon K. and Annie Pyles.

18. Old Methodist Parsonage

The old Southern Methodist Episcopal Parsonage was built in 1903 by Scott Beall, Charles Sellman and Frank Money. The land was purchased from the adjoining farm of Philip Mossburg. The two-story house with Victorian influences was used as the parsonage from 1904 until 1959. The rear addition was built in memory of Mr. and Mrs. Charles Bartgis financed by Della Darby. Previously Sunday School classes were held in this building, but the Poolesville Day Care Center now occupies the building.

19. Bessie Grubb House

This house was built c. 1912 for Miss Bessie Grubb where she ran a boarding house for many years. After her death in 1957 Dr. and Mrs. Byron D. White purchased the house and had it converted into two apartments. Currently Susan Mundy and Shelley Metcalf are the owners.

20. Charles and Fannie Elgin House

Built in 1918 for Charles W. and Fannie J. Elgin, this Colonial Revival style house is two and a half stories with a wrap around porch. Charles was the co-owner of Elgin's General Merchandise and Drug Store. Currently Edward Wesley "Buddy" Maxwell stores antiques here and farms the land behind it. He resides in Brookeville. This side view photograph was taken in 1941 and shows the dormers, back porch, and rear chimney.

21. Elgin House

Charles Sellman was in the process of building this Colonial two-story brick house when he passed away. After his death the Elgins hired B. Z. Harding in 1947 to complete the home. Mr. Harding was also building the Upper Montgomery County Volunteer Fire Department at this time. Charles Elgin was a former mayor of Poolesville and lived here until his death in 1997. His widow, Dorothy Jones Elgin lives here at the present time.

22. Elgin Farm

The tract "Elizabeth's Delight" was purchased in 1760 by John Poole, Sr. from Charles Hoskinson. The property was resurveyed and John's portion was named "Poole's Right." John leased part of his land to Michael Coates, a carpenter, in 1767. The lease stipulated that Mr. Coates was to build a small house, tobacco barn, and plant an apple orchard. After the death of John Poole, Sr. his heirs sold the farm to Philip Mossburg. Mr. Mossburg had the front portion of the house constructed in 1905. The center gable, five bay house is typical of this era. The side features a two-story Victorian style bay window. Beautiful gingerbread trim adorns the full-length front porch. In 1930 the farm was sold to John T. and Edward W. Elgin. It remained in the family until 1977 when the house and two acres were sold to Robert and Iva Rauch. There have been several owners of the house between the Rauch's and the Stypecks including the Royals, the Kings, and Michael and Susan Proser. The present owners are Allan and Kim Stypeck. The photograph was taken in 1940. The remainder of the 176 acres are owned by the Elgin Family Partnership.

23. Second site of Poolesville Baptist Church

Philip Reed lived here and was the postmaster from 1855-1861. The post office was located in his son Benjamin's cabinet shop. Benjamin's sons were painters and plasterers, and their mother had a millinery shop next door. In 1864 William Matthews sold this parcel as lot 2 to the Trustees of the Baptist church: William J. Jones, George D. Powell, John W. Booth, James H. Money, James W. Miles, and Samuel R. White. When the congregation built a church at another location, Thomas Poole purchased this lot and five others adjoining it. In 1906 Florence Poole inherited this lot from Frederick Poole and deeded it to the Maryland Baptist Union Association. The frame church was built in 1914 to serve the eleven remaining members of the congregation. In 1924 the church was dissolved and the building was sold in 1925 to Robert W. Hempstone who operated a silent movie theater here. When "talkies" became prevalent Hempstone closed the theater. The property was sold to Col. Alfred and Louise C. Heiberg on April 8, 1947. Mrs. Heiberg was the former wife of General Douglas MacArthur. The building was remodeled to house several enterprises. The Western Auto supply store is owned and operated by Bill Bliss. John Spellman operates the Poolesville Supply Company and Mark Warner runs the Nationwide Insurance Agency. Also "Bob's Bikes" is located here.

24. site of the Old Hoskinson House

This house was built c. 1860 for Benjamin F. Reed and the addition was constructed at the turn of the twentieth century. Hilleary Hoskinson purchased the property from Henry W. Talbott and Thomas B. Benson. His heirs had various tenants: Thomas Chiswell and his family lived here, then in 1905-6 Estelle F. Hodgson and her daughter Emma rented the house until 1915. The photograph below was taken in the summer of 1905 and shows Dr. Arthur Elgin and John Elgin standing on the porch. The Poolesville Telephone Company was located in this house in 1910. The old house was replaced by the center building shown in the top photograph on the following page. Harry Willard purchased the property and had the two side wings built in 1940. The Montgomery County Health Center was housed in the right wing and Joseph Willard operated a Laundromat and an electrical repair shop here. Tinker's Taxidermy and Old Town Hunting Supply as well as the Teen Center are located in the present building.

25. Melton-Beeding-Poole-Hall House

The log section of the house was built c. 1804 for tailor Raphael Melton who also had a musket pad in the basement which was used to melt lead for making bullets. Located on lot 11 of Whitaker's "Difficulty" this lot was inherited by his daughter Eleanor in 1824. In 1830 Elisha Howard purchased the property and then sold it to Craven P. and Rosetta Lackland Beeding in 1832 who also purchased the adjoining lot from Christina Whitaker Trundle. Beeding had a frame house constructed in 1832 at a cost of $3,000. He furnished it with expensive furniture, a piano, fine china, and purchased a fine carriage, but fell into financial difficulties shortly thereafter. Beeding transferred his property to his wife, Rosetta, and claimed bankruptcy. In 1850 William Dennis and Rebecca Poole purchased the home and two lots. In 1860 Poole purchased lot nine from the estate of Franklin Veirs, son of Sarah Whitaker Veirs and Levi Veirs. From 1869-1889 William Wallace and Avilda A. Poole owned the house and three lots. James F. Poole purchased the home in 1889 and it remained in the Poole family until 1903 when Julius and Margaret Dutrow Hall purchased the property. During the 1930's the Halls boarded teachers and the third two bay section was added at that time. After Margaret's death in 1957 the house passed to their son John who lived here until his death in 1985. Joseph Brenneman, noted preservationist and restorer of historic houses, purchased and renovated the house. This two-story house features heart pine floors, and most of the window panes are original. The foyer is open to the second floor, the fireplace mantle is original, and a chandelier lights the living room. The house is currently owned by Mr. and Mrs. Henry Nessul.

26. Hempstone House

John S. Poole II sold one half acre of "Poole's Right" to Christian T. Hempstone on July 15, 1814. Listed in the 1820 tax assessment with a house on the property, the first log house must have been built around 1815. Christian T. and Mary R. Hempstone sold the property to Daniel Heifner, Sr. [sic]on April 25, 1854. Daniel Heifner and Eliza A. Offutt sold the lot to Thomas Carr Lannan on June 5, 1860. The frame house was built in 1878 for Vernon and Ann Elizabeth Poole Hempstone. The house was owned and occupied by their son Robert until his death in 1970. Presently Edward Wesley "Buddy" Maxwell owns this house.

27. Benson-Pyles-Beall House

This home was built for Thomas and Susan Benson c. 1840. After the death of Thomas Benson, Susan remarried to Richard Pyles. The two-story frame house has a stone foundation, two bays, single story front porch. Jennie Pyles and her two brothers John and William Pyles remained in the house. Jennie was a dressmaker and John was a cobbler. Raymond and Lucy Beall owned and lived in this house from the 1940's until the 1980's. Charles and Doris Glass purchased the home and sold it to Monte and Divine Bledsoe, the present owners.

28. Mount Pleasant

The log house was built for Alexander Whitaker in 1740. The mill was operational by 1783 and was powered by a stream on the property. An addition to the house was built in 1796 and is pictured below. The first floor had a parlor, bedroom, dining room, pantry, and a staircase. The windows were placed high to prevent his servants from seeing him playing cards. Several more bedrooms were located upstairs. As was the custom of the time, the kitchen was located in a separate stone building. The floors were flat stone slabs, and a flag stone walk spanned the ten feet from the kitchen to the main house. The large open fireplace had iron cranes for cooking vessels and baking shelves. A weaving room was also located one the first floor of the kitchen building, with servants quarters above these two rooms. Philip Cissell purchased the home and acreage in approximately 1820. His brother William and wife Rachel Sarah Williams Cissel received the property from Philip. Their thirteen children were raised there, and many of the family were buried in the cemetery on the grounds; although the stones were moved to Monocacy Cemetery on September 1, 1896. John Robert and Laura L. Wright lived here after the Cissells. He was a barber as well as a farmer. Lee and Mabel Walden bought the place from the heirs of the Wrights and restored the house. After various interim tenants, William and Ann Willard purchased the property.

29. Killmain II

Originally part of the 1,300 acre land grant of Daniel Carroll, this property was parceled from Killmain. The three-story brick house was built c. 1812 for Ludwick Young, Jr. Off the center hall is the dining room and the parlor. Both rooms have high ceilings and the hand carved mantles are original. Hezekiah Trundle had William Matthews of Poolesville survey the 646 acres in July of 1849. Basil B. Pleasants of Virginia purchased 123 acres of the property in 1840 and an additional 523 acres at a cost of $6,800 in 1850. He was a member of the Society of Friends, and a small Meeting House built of chinked logs covered with mortar was constructed near the road. During a financially challenging period two Friends loaned him money for his mortgage payments in 1867. Basil attempted human flight from this home sitting high on a knoll by jumping off the roof while wearing giant wings. Area residents who had assembled to witness the event watched Basil fall to the front yard, breaking his leg in the attempt. He also failed to keep the farm and John F. Waesche became the owner in 1873, selling it to Benson Talbot soon afterward. William F. Seymour, a Georgetown milliner, purchased 125 acres and the house for $7,500 in 1880 for his daughter Alice and son-in-law Dr. Wilfred F. McLeod. John Waesche again bought the farm in 1889 following the death of William F. Seymour for Waesche's son Richard who lived there with his wife for many years. In 1940 his widow sold the home to Claude Livingston who purchased additional adjoining acreage. In 1946 the 132 acre farm was purchased by Captain L. A. Abercrombie, USN. In 1993 the Jamison Real Estate Company restored the house and it is currently rented to Tim Thew.

30. Killmain

"Killmain" was a land grant of 1,300 acres patented to Daniel Carroll in 1735. In 1751 the stone house and land was left to Daniel Carroll II's three daughters, Mary, Eleanor, and Elizabeth. In 1772 Richard Bennett Hall purchased the property and left it to his son Richard Lowe Hall. The interior featured primitive wooden floors, hand-made glass window panes and an ell built of stone at a later date.Ludwick and Catherine Shafer Young moved from Hagerstown, purchased the property c. 1813, raised their family here, and were buried in the family plot on the premises. Their son David inherited the house and land after his father's death in 1879. David's son Isaac was the subsequent owner, and Isaac's daughter, Verlinda Lucretia Young Clagett, was the last of the family to live here. Charles W. Oxley bought the remaining 173 acre farm and sold it to Adam and Margaret Neel Shannon in 1927. Because of a crack in the wall of the house, the Jacobsons had the house demolished, buried in what had been the basement, and a new house built on the site. The property is currently owned by Mr. Barge. The stones were moved to Monocacy on November 12, 1896.

31. East Oaks

Originally this was part of "Killmain," a 1,300 acre grant which was patented to Daniel Carroll in 1735. This 278 acre parcel was conveyed to his daughter who married Richard Bennett Hall. Hall conveyed the property to his son Richard Lowe Hall who sold it to Ludwick Young. When his son Henry married Margaret Chiswell the two-story brick house was built for them c. 1823 and called Little Oak Manor. The house is situated on a hill with a lovely view of the surrounding landscape. On the lower floor are the parlor, hall and dining room. The hall leads to the terrace. The second floor contains the bedrooms and fireplaces. In 1865 the property passed to Henry Young, Jr. and his wife Martha Cissell Young. Martha sold it in 1909 to George W. Brewer. In 1916 James and Irea Clothier purchased the farm where they prospered until James death. The farm was sold in 1942 to Daniel J. and Catherine Anne Bishop Callahan. Mr. Callahan was the vice president of Riggs National Bank. The present owners are Dr. Alan B. and Betty Weintraub. Modern plumbing has been added and the slave quarters have been converted into a guest house.

32. Stout House

Frame, off the road, not far, has been cleared, go past modern house after rectory abt 1/4 mile. Robert and Claudia C. Offutt Stout raised four children here. Mr. Stout was the principal of Poolesville High School from 1906 to 1921. He had an apple orchard on the farm. William & Doris McLain purchased the property and sold it to Steve and Susan Goldberg.

33. McDonough-Allnutt House

This property was conveyed to Joshua and J. Mary Acker McDonough on August 29, 1833 from Benjamin and Anne Poole. Joshua McDonough built the house and had his wheelwright shop here. His son William R. was a year old when they moved here from Loudoun County, Virginia, but the other children, Caroline, Catherine and Thomas were born here. On January 9, 1849 the property was sold to James N. Allnutt and McDonough moved his home and business to the east end of town. Poolesville Postmaster William W. Metzger moved the Poolesville Post Office here in 1861. It was here until 1869, after which Dr. Eugene Jarboe and Dr. Samuel B. Milford had their dental office in this house. Frank and Susie Davis lived here before moving to the home on Westerly Avenue which they remodeled. When Isaac and Betty Darby Fyffe acquired the adjoining property they rented this building to various tenants, but the house was demolished in the 1940's.

34. Metzger House-St. Peter's Rectory

This parcel was once lot #5, part of Alexander Whitaker's tract "Difficulty." His son George W. Whitaker inherited the property in 1824. In 1833 it was sold to Benjamin and Ann Poole who sold it to George and Sarah Metzger in 1833. One section of the house may date to this ownership. Each two bay section is frame construction with the entrance in the side of the house. After the death of William W. Metzger in 1905 his widow Amanda lived here for a short time and then it was purchased by Isaac and Betty Darby Fyffe in 1907. In 1947 they sold to Colonel Alfred and Mrs. Louise C. Heiberg, the former Mrs Douglas MacArthur. In 1948 they sold to E. Otho and Clara W. Peters who remained here until 1964. R. Cromwell and Mary Margaret Allnutt Cromwell purchased the house in 1964 and rented it out. A rear addition enlarged the living space in the house during this time period. Afterward, St. Peter's Episcopal Church acquired the house so that the rectory could be closer to the Church. The Reverend Stephen and Kathleen Hayward reside here presently.

35. St. Peter's Episcopal Church

The congregation originally worshiped at the Monocacy Chapel of Ease in Beallsville. The damage to the 130 year old building during the Civil War was serious, and the new building was built in Poolesville by Franklin Viers between 1845 and 1847 of brick. The church was 33 by 46 feet, with three Gothic windows on each side and two in the front. St. Peter's cost $2,000 and is one of the oldest churches in continual use for that purpose. The land was lots six and seven purchased by Frederick, Thomas and William Poole from Eleanor Whitaker Cissell in 1834 for $140. They transferred the deed to the Vestry of the Church. The consecration service took place on February 28, 1850 with Bishop R. Whittingham officiating. The former slave gallery doorway can still be seen, although it has been bricked up. The wooden altar was made by William T. Hilton in Barnesville. The original wooden steeple was blown down in a storm and replaced with a brick tower. In 1890 a chancel and vestibule were added to replace the robing room. Another room above this was used for a school for girls taught by Miss Ella Towles, daughter of the rector in the 1870's. Electricity was installed in 1928, and choir pews were added in 1936. In 1939 and oil burner replaced the coal furnace and the following year a Hammond organ was purchased. The parish hall was purchased and moved from St. Timothy's in Anacostia, D. C. at a cost of $11,500. In 1958 additional land for a parking lot was purchased for $600. The church was remodeled in 1972 and a brick parish hall was built in 1984 at a cost of $450,000.

The rectors serving this church have been:

Rev. Asa S. Colton	1850-1854
Rev. Russell	1854-1860
Rev. William Trapnell	1860-1868
Rev. J. D. McCabe	1869-1873
Rev. John Towles	1874-1877
Rev. Henry Thomas	1878-1888
Rev. Walter P. Griggs	1890-1911
Rev. William R. Bushby	1912-1912
Rev. C. D. Lafferty	1913-1915
Rev. A. J. Smith	1915-1918
Rev. E. P. Wroth	1920-1922
Rev. B. Griffiths	1923-1926
Rev. George C. Shears	1927-1928
Rev. Guy H. Crook	1929-1942
Rev. Herbert Jukes	1944-1950
Rev. Benjamin W. Nevitt	1951-1952
Rev. Carter Gillis	1952-1959

Rev. John Williams   1960-1968
Rev. Ronald Heister   1969-1980
Rev. Donald Gausby   1981-1982
Rev. Steven H. Hayward 1982-

Memorials

The brass altar cross was given in memory of William Wallace Poole, Superintendent of Sunday School Classes 1870-1900. The wide vases were also given in his memory.
The brass candlesticks were given in memory of Newton Emmert by his daughter, Mary Emmert.
The brass vases were given in memory of Dr. Edward Wootton 1839-1910.
The low brass vases were given in memory of John Moore by his family.
The Missal was given by the Women's League in 1912.
The walnut collection plates were given in memory of Joseph Pyles by his widow.
The church flag and United States flag were given in memory of Dr. Joseph White by his widow.
The lectern was given in honor of Richard Poole 1843-1906.
The pulpit was given in memory of Rosalie Poole by her husband Rev. Henry Thomas Poole on June 12, 1905.
The church bell, cast in England, was a gift of Rev. William Trapnell from a church in Southern Maryland.

Windows

Moses and the Ten Commandments- in memory of William D. and Rebecca Poole 1804-1869 and 1808-1880 respectively.
Good Shepherd-in memory of Frederick Sprigg and Mary D. Poole 1809-1888 and 1812-1883 respectively.
Cross and Lilies-in memory of Martha Poole 1830-1888.
Ascension-in memory of Sallie Cummings Griggs 1864-1896 by her husband Rev. Walter P. Griggs.
Gethsemane-in memory of Virginia Poole Wallace 1909-1969
Jesus Blesses the Children-in memory of Peggy Angel Wood.
Calling of St. Peter-in memory of Rev. Walter and Anna Poole Williams
Christian Soldier-in memory of Rev. Carter Stellwagon Gillis 1907-1960.
The Nativity Scene was given in memory of Charles W. Elgin, Sr. 1915-1997.

St. Peter's Episcopal Church

36. Hoskinson House

Originally part of lot #1 of Peter's "Forest" this was lot eight of Alexander Whitaker's "Difficulty" and divided again in 1828. The lot was further divided in 1835 with 5/8 of the property purchased by Hilleary and Dorcas Ann Hoskinson. Built in 1849 this two-story, three bay brick house with Federal detailing exhibits the economic prosperity enjoyed in Poolesville during the mid-1800's. In 1851 the property was sold to Ann R. W. Johnson. Thomas Hoskinson had the frame ell added in the 1880's. He owned the house from 1879-1931. It was white washed during modern times. The present owner is Dr. James M. Buchanan. Between St. Peter's Episcopal Church and this house once stood the wheelwright and blacksmith shops and home of William Walter. On the other side once stood the house and tailor shop of John W. Hall. Built in 1848, the shop became a millinery shop run by his widow after in 1924. She then married Murrel J. Morningstar and the house became a double rental property. Carrie Frye, a dressmaker, lived in one section and Mr. and Mrs. David Ward lived in the other. Mr. Ward operated the garage across the street until 1976. The house was burned as a fire drill for the Upper Montgomery Volunteer Fire Department in 1976. The bank was built on this site in 1978.

37. 1785 House

This property was purchased by James Soper in 1806. The farm was called "Difficulty" and contained 231 acres. James' widow Marien sold the property to Alexander Whitaker shortly before Whitaker's death. Whitaker willed the farm to his children, each were to receive two of the sixteen lots. A portion of the present house was built on Whitaker's lot #1. Richard Poole had the brick two-story house built c. 1830, a log kitchen was attached to the rear of the east building until 1960. If the log building was built in 1785 it could explain the derivation of the name of the house. The third floor window on the east side contains a large fanlight. The addition was built as a separate house, but later it was adjoined by an interior doorway. Two unusual windows contain four panes each with two sections side by side. Richard Poole died in 1832 and the property was purchased by Gerhart Metzger. It remained in the Metzger family until 1877 when Airy Ann and Columbia Jones purchased it. From 1924 - 1936 Anna L. Darby owned the house. She sold it in 1936 to Harry L. and Delma D. Willard. In 1949 Charlotte Guilford Mulhofer purchased the house but sold it in 1950 to Isabell Sprigg who owned it until 1960. Thomas and Laura Conlon purchased the house and sold it to their son-in-law Charles Jamison in 1960. Frank Flower purchased it in 1961 and had it painted white. John Sumner and Peggy Wood bought the house in 1961. The present owner is William R. Roberts, an attorney. Pictured on the following page are the log section of the house and in the lower photograph, the outbuldings.

38. Dr. Thomas Poole House

Built in 1835 for Thomas and Sarah Ann E. Poole, this three-story, three bay Georgian town house was their home until her death in 1844. The entrance features fluted columns and arch over the door's fanlight. The elegant stairway has a mahogany banister and the ten foot ceilings are adorned with rosette centers. In 1846 he married Evelina Wailes Hyde and their daughter Alice Poole was born here. The Federal style architecture is set off by a fanlight above the door. Alice Poole Gott, wife of Dr. Gott, inherited the house and added the two-story east wing as a doctor's office in 1865. The Gotts lived here until 1913. Charles Sellman lived here for a for a short period, selling to in 1929 to William Wallace and Carrie Lucile Williams Poole. Mr. and Mrs. Daniel Dollarhide lived in this house when he was the principal of Poolesville High School. George A. and Effie Moran Meerdink purchased the house in 1936 and sold it in 1951. Dr. Arthur Mann had his office in the extension, after which Dr. Ralph Williams practiced dentistry there. It was operated as a restaurant in the 1970's under the names King's Head Tavern, Country Peddler Inn and Cross Country Inn. The Historic Medley District purchased the home, repaired it and then sold it to Mr. and Mrs. Stanley Deets.

39. Frederick Poole House

In August of 1819 George and Agnes Peter sold this parcel of "Forest" to Robert Willson. Built c. 1819 for Robert Willson this house is mentioned in the 1820 tax assessment. In 1824 Willson also purchased lots 3, 4, and 5 from Ignatius Davis who had purchased them from Major George Peter. Originally five bays, the two-story brick house has been enlarged to seven bays, at which time the third chimney was added. In 1835 Willson's son-in-law Frederick Sprigg Poole and wife Mary Tillard Douglas Willson Poole purchased the house from the estate of her father who had died in 1833. Frederick was the postmaster from 1839-1854. Colonel Edward Baker chose to use this house as his headquarters prior to the Battle of Ball's Bluff. His body was brought here following the battle, before being sent to the Presidio in San Francisco. At this time there was a square Federal style entrance porch which was replaced by the full length porch. Richard Poole, son of Frederick, lived here with his wife Florence Poole. Their daughter Frances and her husband William Williams purchased the house in 1931. Retired PHS principal Harry Rhodes boarded here from 1935-1938 and recalls paying $25.00 a month for room and board. Dr. Julian Freeman purchased the property and had the rear-ell built to accommodate four apartments and the house was covered in pebble dash at this time. Dr. Freeman had the brick post office and restaurant constructed where Leo Bassett presently operates Bassett's Restaurant in the entire building. Benjamin and Linda Molayem are the present owners of the Frederick Poole House.

40. General Store and Post Office

One of the old stores of Poolesville which was located next to Wootton's also housed the post office at one time. The old side walks were wooden planks along the dirt road and were built before 1860. Pictured below are John Thomas Elgin, Julius Hall, and Edward Wootton Elgin. The bay window showcases the fine merchandise in stock for the shoppers' selection, and the left side of the store carried machinery and parts needed by farmers. Men gathered on the front porch to discuss the weather, politics and the happenings of the day before heading home for supper.

41. Wootton and Elgin's Store

This lot was sold by Richard and Florence Poole in 1896 and Albert Wootton's 1897 store stood on this site. The photograph below was taken in 1905 and shows Frank I. Davis, standing, and William Butler, seated on the left. In 1915 it was sold to James E. and Olive Pyles and it burned in the 1923 fire. Harry Willard built a large building on this site which housed the Poolesville Post Office when Ernest Willard was the postmaster. Carl Fisher had a general merchandise store with Zachariah M. Compher's meat market located here, too. Mr. Willard held Saturday night dances over the store and folks came from all around to enjoy the fun. Selby's Market occupied the site from 1936 until they relocated in 1996.

Selby's Market

Bassett's Restaurant

42. Spurrier's Store

Clara B. Hall deeded this lot which was part of "Forest" to Sadie Williams in 1906 who conveyed it to Howard W. Spurrier in 1907. The store carried shoes, hats, coats, material and other goods. This store burned in the 1923 fire and a new store was built. G. Robert Gray operated a general merchandise and shoe store here before Roy and Frances Selby purchased this property and attached it to his store.

43. Confectionery Shop

Pictured below are the stores in the business district of Poolesville c. 1890: Fannie Money Morrison's house is on the extreme left, then Hoskinson's Store, Wootton and Elgin's Store, General Store and Poolesville Post Office, and Charles Norris' house. One of the enterprises at that time was the confectionery shop. It was operated by Carl Fisher and Jim Brooks. After graduating from Poolesville High School they opened a small store for ice cream and lemonade in an old house built in the late 1870's. Jim Brooks left the business and became a farmer. The store burned in the 1923 fire.

44. Williams Store

This lot was formerly occupied by Hoskinson's General Merchandise Store. Susan R. Reed conveyed the property to Dorcas Hoskinson on February 29, 1876. It was later deeded to William C. Hoskinson and on July 20, 1909 to Thomas Hoskinson. The fire on August 16, 1923 started in this building and $6,000 worth of stock was lost. The loss of the building was estimated at $3,000. Harry and William Williams built the present building in 1927 which is now owned by Ida Williams. The first floor is occupied by Crafts-A-Plenty operated by Reva Hoewing. The second floor has been converted into several apartments.

45. White House-Merchant's Hotel

Samuel Daniel Trundle purchased this lot from the estate of Major George Peter in 1829. Dr. Stephen Newton Chiswell White married Ann Belt Trundle, daughter of S. Daniel Trundle and the lot was conveyed to them after her father's death in 1831. In 1833 the late Federal style house and office was built for Dr. Stephen Chiswell White. In 1860 Dr. White died and Ann sold the house to Charles E. M. Kohlhoss. In the 1880's the house was converted into the Merchant's Hotel. The two-story brick east wing dates to this time period. An advertisement for the Merchant's Hotel states that it is conveniently located, has large airy, newly papered rooms furnished and everything. Rates were $1.00-$1.50 per day, with Table Board $3.00 to $3.50 per week. Permanent Guests $4.00-$5.00 per week. Free bus to and from Barnesville Station for regular guests. Good Stabling attached. The Kohlhoss shoe shop was located next to the house. Charles E. and Emma Kohlhoss lived here until 1968. He operated a Ford dealership and the Poolesville Motor Company next to their house. Charles E. Kohlhoss, Jr. subsequently ran the business and his widow, Winnie, now rents the garage to Poolesville Auto and Performance. The house which had been vacant since 1971 was torn down in 1985 to increase the parking facilities for the garage.

46. Lyles-Poole-Watkins House

This two and a half story house was built in c. 1860 on a sandstone foundation. The original wood has been covered over with vinyl siding. The center gable balances the center door in the middle of the five bays. The one acre lot had been part of Thomas Peter's land and was sold to Robert Lyles in 1847. At the time of Robert's death Juliet, Robert J., Dr. Richard and wife Susan Lyles were also living here. In 1869 William Wallace and Avilda Poole purchased the property. William operated a store in a small building west of his house. Dr. James Edwin and Ruth Roberts Pyles lived here and he operated a drug store at the corner of Elgin Road and Fisher Ave. The present owner is Betty Watkins.

47. Elias Price House

This two and a half story frame house with center gable was built in the 1850's. Daniel Price sold the property to Elias Price on June 23, 1868. Elias Price was a member of "Chiswell's Exiles" and the Co. B of the 35th Battalion Army of Virginia. At the Battle of Brandy Station he received a serious wound in this leg. The following day it was amputated at the thigh, and he never fully recovered. In 1909 Clarence Price purchased the house from Mr. Robertson. Clara, Cora, Ida, and Gertrude Price lived in this house for many years. Miss Clara Price ran a millinery shop in former Baptist Church building next door and later was clerk to the Commissioners of Poolesville. The present owner is Robert Ladd and the house has been renovated to accommodate several apartments.

48. Baptist Church-Norris Building

This building was constructed in 1864-5 for the members of the Baptist Church. The brick church was 25 x 40 feet and cost $1,200. The church was dedicated on May 28, 1865 and G. N. Samson delivered the dedicatory sermon, assisted by Elders White and Adams. The congregation was formed when nine families of the Rockville congregation withdrew on November 5, 1860 and formed a congregation in Poolesville. They met in the Presbyterian Church until August of 1863 when the church was used for a Union soldiers hospital. Assistant pastor Reverend John William Booth was also the school teacher and arranged for the congregation to meet in the schoolhouse during the construction of their own building. Elder White served as the first minister and resigned in September of 1865. The other pastors include: H. J. Chandler, Mr. Davis, Rev. T. E. Woodson, who pastored both the Germantown and the Poolesville Churches in 1875, Mr. Kearns, and when Rev. Calvin L. Amy came in 1878 he noted that there were only 24 members. Reverend R. E. Hatcher followed him in 1880 and the congregation had shrunk to only 15 members. In the 1930's and early 1940's Clara Price ran a millinery store here. The building later was purchased by Charles W. Norris who operated the Norris Fuel Oil Company and Norris Building Supply here. Steve and Susan Goldberg now own the building. Poolesville Quality Cleaners operates their dry cleaning business here presently, and Hearthside Antiques Store is located next door.

49. Reddick House

George and Addie Spurrier Reddick purchased property from the heirs of George Peter on September 28, 1892. They had a house built shortly thereafter and in 1909 sold a parcel of the property to the Poolesville Baptist Church. Mrs. Reddick lived here until 1961. Howard Spurrier lived here with his sister until he built a house following his marriage to Ethel Grubb. The house was then rented to various occupants. The house was demolished to make room for the Chesapeake and Potomac Telephone Company Building. The Poolesville Post Office is located on the adjoining property.

50. Young House

Built c. 1909 for Dr. Samuel B. Milford, it was then occupied by Della Young and her mother until 1964. Various families lived here following her death including: Thomas and Emily Lydanne, Mary Emmert and her father, Mary Buxton, George and Bettie Brewer and Mrs. Elaine Cook who ran a dance studio. The house was sold to Jay Swartzman and burned by the Upper Montgomery County Volunteer Fire Department as a drill. Mr. Swartzman then built the Poolesville Beer, Wine, and Deli Store on the site in 1975.

51. site of Arthur Fletchall House

This former two and a half story, five bay house was built for Arthur Poole and Lulu Hall Fletchall c. 1880. The front porch was ornamented with Victorian period gingerbread work. Other features include two chimneys, center gable, and the west side had a Victorian bay window. Mr. Fletchall was the postmaster from 1894-1898 and 1914-1922. He also served on many church committees at the Methodist Episcopal Church South. The Fletchall's daughter Clarine married Charles W. Woodward who taught at Briarley Hall Military Academy and later became the Chief Justice of the Montgomery County Circuit Court. The couple lived here with the Fletchalls for a time. Their sons were Judge Charles W. Woodward, Jr. and Dr. Arthur F. Woodward. One of his grandsons, Patrick Woodward, also became a judge. Mrs. Helen Loftus purchased the house and rented it out. After it was vacated, it was used as a haunted house at Halloween before becoming unsafe. At Helen Loftus' request, the house was burned as a fire drill for the Upper Montgomery County Volunteer Fire Department in 1983.

52. Site of Barnard T. Norris House

The log section of this house was built in 1830 for Barnard T. Norris after his marriage to Ann Fyffe earlier that year. The three-story white frame house was built in 1863 and had five bays and a center gable. Mr. Norris' cabinet shop was located next door. In 1888 he willed the house to his son James Norris. The house was later lived in by Mrs. Mollie Fyffe and her daughter Aldah for many years. Other owners include Dr. Joseph M. and Creszensa L. White, Glen and Nancy Goldburn, Mr. and Mrs. Roy De La Vergne, and Charles E. Jr. and Winifred Kohlhoss. The house was sold to the Magruder Corporation who had it burned down as a fire drill by the Upper Montgomery County Volunteer Fire Department. This site now has a modern shopping center.

53. John Fyffe House

The land for this house was parceled from the property on the preceding page when Mollie Fyffe owned the land. The house was built in 1936 by T. W. "Brownie" Brown of Comus. John and Martha Cooley Fyffe boarded school teachers and raised two children here.

54. site of Lutie Hempstone House

This house may have been built for John T. Norris in 1859. The two-story three bay frame house had two end chimneys and the front porch featured decorative cornice work. Lutie Norris Hempstone lived here until her death in 1944. There were several owners during the next forty years. In October 1989 the house was torn to make way for the McDonalds which presently occupies this site. It is owned and operated by Bryan and Cathy Cleghorn.

55. site of Hall House

This two-story Colonial Revival house was built in 1890. The frame house features three bays on the second floor, and four on the first floor with an offset doorway. The house was built for Thomas Randolph II and Beulah Bouic White Hall. Thomas was a Justice of the Peace and tried local cases. Beulah's father was a Baptist minister and the first Superintendent of Montgomery County Public Schools. Their son Thomas Randolph Hall III was born here in 1907. He graduated from Northwestern University and spoke fluent German and Russian. He was with General Clay in Office of Strategic Information in World War II. Roy and Mollie Bodmer lived here followed by Lawrence and Mary Guthrie, who lived here for many years. This house was located diagonally across from Meadlowlark Inn and was burned as a drill for the Upper Montgomery Volunteer Fire Department to make room for the shopping center.

56. Rozier Bodmer House

The land for this house was parceled from the Jacob Bodmer property on the following page. The house was built at a cost of $3,000 for Charles Rozier and Zada Ryman Bodmer. Mr. Bodmer was a veteran of World War I. The Poolesville Band rehearsed in the basement of this house for many years.

57. Jacob Bodmer House

On December 10, 1908 Jacob and Carrie Melissa Wiles Bodmer purchased this property from John H. Spurrier. The house was built c. 1910 and the rear addition was added at a later time. Mr. Bodmer had a shoe repair shop and was also the first rural carrier on the Poolesville route. This two and half story, five bay, brick home was purchased from their heirs in the early 1940's by the Butlers and Vandercooks. Anna F. Vinci Slaysman is the current owner. The rear ell has front porches running the length of both floors.

58. Jones-Bernsdorff House

Sarah Elizabeth Poole Jones, daughter of John Poole II and Priscilla Woodward Sprigg Poole, inherited this property which at that time totaled 354 acres. The attractive stone house was built for Isaac and Sarah Elizabeth Poole Jones in 1835. After Isaac's death Sarah married his brother Thomas Lloyd Jones in 1852. The west wing addition was constructed in 1860 following a 1852 fire in the house. Mrs. Jones died in 1905 and her daughter Priscilla John Jones continued to live here. Other owners of the land include: Harry Willard, Henry J. Norris, Walter B. Fyffe, and Cleveland Cromwell, and Mr. and Mrs. Chauncey Snow in 1938. In 1944 Colonel Fletcher F. and Jane Bernsdorff purchased the house which is now on the National Register of Historic Places. Handsome stone outbuildings and a barn are located in the rear.

59. Hughes-Leapley House

The original section of this house is log. It was built for Joseph Adolphus Hughes
c. 1864. The frame section of the house was built c. 1874 with a central chimney
and center gable. The three bay addition more than doubled the former size of the
house. The windows were set low to enable their son Dolie, who was confined to
a wheelchair, to see out. Catherine "Jennie" Leapley lived here until she died in
1953. The present owners are Franklin and Marilyn Banach.

60. Norris-Chiswell House

Built c. 1882 for Henry J. and Laura B. Imlay Norris, this two-story frame house was later owned and occupied by George Chiswell. His daughter Catherine Chiswell worked as a telephone operator in Poolesville for the Hodgsons before marrying Lloyd Grubb. The present owners are David and Kathleen McNamara. The lower section of the chimney appears to be constructed of stone, while the section above the second story of the house has been replaced by bricks. The three bay house has a wrap around front porch and several additions have been through the years.

61. Spurrier-Munger House

This two and a half story, five bay frame house was built for John H. Spurrier c. 1904. It was sold to Jacob Bodmer where he lived until he built the house across the road. It was sold to John B. Munger and his grandson Fred Munger Campbell and wife Jessie Bodmer Campbell were the next owners. Presently the house is owned by Henry T. and Kathleen Varno.

62. Meadow Lark Inn

The present structure was built in 1861, [1840?] as the home of Samuel Cator. Mr. Cator was the blacksmith and postmaster from 1861-1877. His shop was located behind the house. Mary Elgin Mann purchased the house in 1910. Mrs. Mann's brother Dr. Arthur G. and his wife Diana Carpenter Elgin moved here from New York and their sons Cliff and Charles were born here. Charles was the postmaster from 1940-1973 and the mayor of Poolesville from 1978-1992. The restaurant was opened in 1963 and several alterations have taken place to accommodate guests. The current owners are Michael and Trudy Zirpolo.

63. Plater-Hauck House

Part of Major George Peter's property "Forest" this parcel adjoins "Poole's Hazard." The lots were subdivided by Joseph Poole and sold to John Poole Thomas Plater, a United States Representative who had the house built c. 1798. William Riney leased this house from Thomas Plater, son of Maryland Governor Plater. Riney kept a tavern here from 1800-1803. Mr. Taylor and then later Henry Fowler kept the tavern in the 1820's when the path of Main Street was relocated. In 1830 the property was described as two acres with a frame house twenty-eight by sixteen feet, a kitchen sixteen feet square, a stable ten feet square and an orchard with twelve peach trees, one apple tree and four cherry trees. The fence encompassed three-quarters of an acres. Samuel Cator purchased "Peter's Forest" in 1850 from the heirs of Thomas Plater and located his blacksmith shop across the road. Later owners include Dr. Samuel B. and Betty Byrd Milford, Alf and Louise Heiberg, Mr. and Mrs. Edwin Tillack and presently Paul and Betty B. Hauck.

64. Talbott-Willard-Cubitt House

Coxen's Road formerly ran from the John Poole House to Meadow Lark Inn. Joseph Poole subdivided his land and sold this lot, lot 3, to his son Benjamin Poole in 1806. The one and a half story frame house was built on lot 3, where the Willard House now stands, in 1866. Miss Sallie Talbott was living there in 1867. In 1903 Silas Young Browning owned the house. Harry Willard had the house moved on rollers by two steam tractors to its' present location in 1912. The Thomas Cator House, which had formerly been on this foundation, had burned to the ground. In 1931 Isaac and Edna Lee Dodd Cubitt purchased the house and lived here until 1975. The current owners are Paul R. and Claudia Shibelski.

65. Joseph Poole-Money-Hersperger House

In 1805 the cabin and lot five were conveyed from John Poole to Joseph Poole, Sr. and the following year the four acre lot was conveyed from Joseph Poole, Sr. to Samuel Poole. The left section of the house was built of brick in 1828. Hilleary Jarvis, one of Poolesville's early schoolmasters, purchased the lot on July 30, 1830. In 1848 Elizabeth Pearce Jarvis, widow of Hilleary T. Jarvis, inherited the property. Her daughter, Rose Anna Jarvis Money, widow of James H. Money, had lived here most of her life and raised her seven children in this house. She inherited the house in 1866. After her death George Willard lived here before the property was sold in 1920 to two of Rose Anna's children: Frank J. Money and Mary F. Money Morrison. They in turn sold it to Charles C. Money in 1927. Ethel Money Jones inherited the property from her father in 1928 and sold it to Marian Lindsey Shears who had the frame addition constructed in 1930. She owned it until 1944 when it was sold to Virginia Hersperger. Rande and Laura Davis in purchased the home in 1998.

66. Beall House

This was lot 6 and was deeded to William Poole, the son of Joseph Poole, Sr. Charles E. and Laura V. Poole sold it to W. Scott and Melissa A. Beall. The house was built by W. Scott Beall c. 1893 and appears to have two sections each having two bays. The frame house is currently stained with the shutters and porch painted. Howard and Alice Beall Frye lived here for many years. The current owner is Jack Stringer, nephew of Alice Beall Frye.

67. Willard House

This Colonial Revival frame house was built by Harry Willard in 1913. The three-story house features four dormers, a central chimney, Victorian bay with gable and a wrap-a-round porch. Mr. Willard married Delmah Dutrow and raised two children here: Helen Willard Pumphrey and Dewalt Joseph Willard, Sr. The current occupant is Mrs. Helen Willard Pumphrey.

68. Elias Beall and Compher House

This two-story brick home was built for Elias Beall c. 1910. His son, Will Beall, lived there for many years. Will's sister, Ruth, married Zachairah M. Compher and lived here in later years. She taught first grade in the Poolesville School for forty-two years. A barber shop was located here which was operated by John Wright and Oliver Soper. Part of the building was remodeled to include two apartments. M. Olivia Green, a retired teacher from Poolesville High School, formerly lived in one of the apartments. Paul and Emma Welsh are the current owners and Mrs. Welsh's mother, Mrs. Madeline Hall lives with them.

69. site of the Century Hotel

When Coxen's Road's path was altered, the present triangular shaped lot was created. The lot containing "Old Hotel and Garden" was originally part of "Poole's Hazard." The Century Hotel was the first building on this site in 1826. Referred to as a tavern kept by William O. West in the road petition of 1827, it was later part of a larger inn run by Richard Spates. It is reported to have had a pump which supplied superior quality water. In 1879 the building was occupied by Mrs. Smith who ran a store here. In 1888 a Y. M. C. A. chapter was organized and met here, but the building burned down in 1900.

70. Town Hall

This lot was deeded to the Poolesville National Bank from Richard and Ann Estelle Owens on May 29, 1908 and construction began that year. Howard W. Spurrier was the president with directors J. Furr White, Arthur P. Fletchall, John A. Jones, DeWalt J. Willard, William C. Hoskinson, Charles W. Morrison, William T. Griffith, J. H. Williams, Clagett C. Hilton, B. W. Walling, A. D. Trundle, James W. Darby, J. E. Pyles and John A. Jones. The bank merged with the Central Trust Company of Maryland which failed in 1930. Many citizens lost their life savings as a result. Several years later a group of Poolesville citizens organized the Poolesville Bank. This state bank later merged with the First National Bank of Maryland. When the bank moved to a new location in 1967 the building was deeded to the town of Poolesville to be used as the town hall. The photograph was taken on April 22, 1918 during the Third Liberty Loan Meeting. The facade of the building has been renovated resulting in the windows being altered and the portico was added at that time.

71. John Poole House

John Poole owned a 15 acre parcel and sold lots to members of his family. This structure was built c. 1793 of chinked logs on a stone foundation. The chimneys have a stone base and brick stacks. One of the oldest buildings in Poolesville, it also served as a combination store. It originally had one room on the ground floor with an attic loft. A lean-to kitchen and fireplace was added in the rear of the house by 1800, and the frame addition was added later. Poole operated the store here until he sold it to Dennis Lackland in 1810. The post office was located here from 1810-1829 with the designation "Poole's Store" until 1819 when "Poolesville" was adopted. The mailman arrived once a week on horse back and his route included Rockville, Darnestown, Poolesville and Leesburg, Virginia. Dennis Lackland did not prosper and the property was purchased by his brother-in-law Ignatius Davis. His nephew and heir, Davis Richardson, sold the property to Martha Pearce Michael who left it to her sister Elizabeth Pearce Jarvis. Mary F. Morrison owned the house in the 1940's. Brooke Jackson owned the house prior to it becoming the headquarters of the Historic Medley District.

72. Viers-Stevens House

Franklin Viers built this two-story, three bay, red brick Federal style townhouse house in 1844. He died the same year, leaving the house to his widow Ann Elizabeth Hall Viers, whose father lived next door. During the Civil War the Confederate forces attacked the signal corps and in the struggle their Captain was killed. The lieutenant escaped to the house and was hidden under a portly servant in the upstairs bedroom. When the house was searched the Union troops looked under the bed while the occupant loudly objected. They did not force her to get up, and the soldier later rejoined his unit. She remarried to William Walter, and left the house to two daughters. One, Lucy Viers, married Charles Sellman and in 1888 they purchased the property which consisted of the brick house of eight rooms, necessary outbuildings, stable, fine well of water and a garden enclosed by a fence. Charles Sellman built many houses in Dickerson and Poolesville. George and Mary Willard owned the building from 1917 to 1948. William and Helen Pendergast owned in from 1949 until 1968. Lawrence Stevens was the next owner. It is currently owned by Nancy Fost who operates the Hand Made'ns Gift Shop.

73. Thomas Hall Building

This land is a parcel from "Poole's Right" which was purchased by Thomas Hall from Henry Collier in 1830. The brick town houses share one common roof and were built in 1830 for Thomas R. Hall. One section had a tailor's shop. The brick meat house, log kitchen, Jacob Bodmer's shoe shop, and a log stable burned in the 1953 fire but are visible in the photograph. At the time of the fire George and Kathryn Willard were living in the addition. John R. Hall purchased part of the property in 1859. His mother was living in the section, and following her death in 1870 he purchased the remaining section. In 1880 John Hall willed it to his daughters Rebecca and Dora who lived in the west section until 1949. Dr. S. B. Milford, D. D. S. had his office in the east section. George and Kathryn Hillard lived here when Charles Jamison purchased in the building in 1953 for his real estate office. The red brick house is currently painted white. Following the retirement of Jacob Bodmer, his shoe shop became vacant, and the men of Poolesville held the pitch card games there.

The Poolesville pitch team was known as the "Ground Hogs" and played against other teams such as the Seneca Muskrats and the Rockville Polecats. The losers treated the winners to an annual dinner. They were so dubbed Ground Hogs because their wives ribbed them about only coming out from their card games long enough to see their shadow. The building burned in the February 6, 1953 fire.

74. Elgin's Drug Store

Collier's Cabinet Shop occupied this site until this building was built in 1910 for Charles W. Elgin's General Merchandise Store. His brother Dr. Arthur G. Elgin soon joined in the business venture adding a pharmacy. The business was then known as Elgin Brothers Drug and General Merchandise until the death of Charles W. Elgin in 1934. Dr. Elgin's son Charles W. Elgin joined the enterprise and became the postmaster of Poolesville in 1940. He had the post office moved into the store at that time. In 1952 Dr. Elgin retired and the store was discontinued. The post office was moved to Cruit's Harness Shop, as it was vacant. The store burned in the 1953 fire.

Above, the Elgin Brother's Store's Soda Fountain. Below, the original I. O. O. F. building. The stage, driven by John Hickman, provided transportation for guests in hotel's to reach Barnesville Station in Sellman, for ladies attending Briarley Hall, and people who came to shop in Poolesville.

75. Odd Fellow's Hall

In the 1820's this was the site of Benjamin and Joseph Pooles' Store. The post office was located here when Joseph Poole was the postmaster 1828-1831. It was sold in 1826 by Ignatius Davis to Henry A. Collier. In 1830 it was sold to Thomas Hall. Lodge 115 of the International Order of Odd Fellows was instituted July 8, 1869. There existed many guilds for men of specific profession and the Odd Fellows were started with the purpose of membership for those whose trade was not included in the other groups, such as Masons. At the time of the founding of this lodge Joseph B. Escaville was the Grand Secretary of the Grand Lodge of Maryland, and he conducted the initial ceremony. After this lodge's charter was surrendered, the Pleasant Hill Lodge 97 moved to Poolesville. The building pictured was built c. 1900 on the same site of the earlier building which was built in 1869. It burned in the February 6, 1953 fire and was rebuilt a third time. A. J. Casale's Barber shop was located in the building and also burned. Currently the barber shop and beauty parlor are located on the first floor, and an apartment is located on the second floor. The barber shop is run by Whitney and Jenni Staver. Brenda Souders operates the beauty parlor. The rent helps fund activities that the Lodge sponsors such as: annual picnic for widows, widowers and orphans, college scholarships, school programs, annual Christmas party for local senior citizens, and other worthy causes. Volunteers staff their thrift shop and donate their time at the Frederick Home. The Lodge meets on second and fourth Tuesdays at 7:30 in the Memorial United Methodist Church.

76. Norris-Morningstar House

Henry Josiah Norris had this house built in the 1880's. The two-and-a-half story frame house has been covered in vinyl siding. The three bay front has a full length porch, and a center gable. A side porch has been added. It was deeded to Murrel J. Morningstar in 1919 after he married June Hall. Morningstar operated a blacksmith shop beside the house. Richard Morningstar operates Morningstar Welding from this location. The house is owned by Richard and Gerald Morningstar and has two apartments.

77. Norris Livery Stable

Off Elgin Road the Norris family operated a livery stable. In addition to caring for horses, renting rigs, and providing transportation, Straub's Carriage Company built carriages here for a time. The photograph shows the livery stable with Charles J. Norris pictured on the left, and stage driver John Hickman on the right. The stage is also pictured just to the right of center. Notice the wooden side walks in the lower left.

78. Norris-Fisher-Hickman House

The three bay center gable frame house was built in 1850 for Charles Norris and later owned by Jacob T. Fisher who operated the livery stable in the rear of the property. The end chimneys balance the gable nicely. John Hickman owned the house and was the stage driver. This house was damaged in a fire and was at risk of demolition when Leo Bassett purchased the home and restored it. The oldest section of the house was built of logs in 1850, the second section was built c. 1900 and consists of two rooms, with two rooms over them. More recent renovations have also been made.

79. site of John O. Merchant House

John O. Merchant purchased property along what was then called Back Street from Mary F. Williams on May 6, 1864. He was a carpenter and undertaker and lived here with his wife Margaret E. Merchant. His shop was located next to the house and for many years he was an associate of Hilton's in Barnesville. After his wife's death in 1883 he built his own coffin and stored it in the parlor of his house for twenty years before being buried in it next to her at Monocacy Cemetery in Beallsville. Dr. Lewis Franklin and Mary Katherine Brooks then purchased the two-story frame house and raised their family here. He was a veterinarian and also owned land across the street which was sold to the Board of Education for the Poolesville High School Campus. The Brooks' house was sold to Mrs. Finegan who rented it to Marion Beall, Jr. After George Hillard bought the house he had the Upper Montgomery County Volunteer Fire Department burn the house as a drill in 1980. In 1981 Mr. Hillard built a new building for his Poolesville Plumbing and rents the second floor to Stanley Janet who is the editor and publisher of the Poolesville Bulletin.

80. Church - Town Hall

Following the split in the Methodist Episcopal denomination the Methodist Episcopal Church members met in this building constructed in the board and batten style. The building is is listed on the 1865 map of Poolesville and the 1879 Atlas. Reverend Morgan and Reverend Randolph Richardson Murphy conducted services here as the membership dwindled. The steward was William Cissell and the Trustees were Samuel C. Cator, William Cissell, and Richard Ashland. After the membership dipped below twelve, the church was dropped from conference records. The building was later used as the town hall. Meetings and elections were held here. St. Peter's Episcopal Church held their Thanksgiving suppers here in the late 1920's and townsfolk were served all the trimmings despite the lack of kitchen facilities. It was used by the high school for plays and other activities before facilities were built at the school. The building burned on March 12, 1931.

81. site of Edward D. Cruitt House

This house was built for Edward D. Cruitt were he ran his harness shop and taught his son Luther the trade. Luther's shop was located on Elgin Road and perhaps got more trade at that location. The next resident was Miss Priscilla John Jones who lived here until 1921. The house was purchased by Honore and Mary White Claggett. The Claggett's moved to Washington, DC in 1928 and the house was vacant except when their son Lawrence came for weekends. The stove exploded on March 12, 1931 killing Lawrence. The house was badly damaged but was partially restored by Harold and Estelle White Brooks. In 1970 the house was burned as a drill for the Upper Montgomery County Volunteer Fire Department.

82. Sellman House

Charles B. Sellman built this house in 1917. Similar to some of his houses built in Dickerson, this house features Victorian influences. The two-story frame construction has a gable over the Victorian bay. Two chimneys flank the Colonial Revival style roof line. The wide wrap-a-round porch is supported by eleven columns. Mr. Sellman and his wife and two sons Charles, Jr. and Richard lived here for many years. The current owners are Thomas and Gina L. Orr.

83. Dr. Wootton House

Dr. Edward Wootton served as a surgeon in the War of 1812, and following the Civil War became one of the leaders of the Democratic Party. This house was built for him c. 1866. In 1868 he was a State Senator and he also jointly owned a warehouse along the Chesapeake and Ohio Canal with Elijah Veirs White. Harry Stevens was the next owner and lived here with his family. Currently Robert and Anna B. Chissler own this property.

84. Darby's Mill

James Washington Darby moved from Buck Lodge to Poolesville to retire, but that didn't last very long. He had this mill built in 1911 and operated it until his death in 1925. A gasoline engine powered the mill which shelled, cracked and ground corn into meal for area farmers. Buck Lodge farmers also had flour ground there. Mary Fyffe owned the building after her grandfather's death and J. Herbert Brown continued the operations until 1929. J. T. Fisher and Son purchased the mill in 1929 and later sold it to William Morris and Duke Ingalls. Ingalls moved and Norris converted the mill into a hardware store. The next owner was Hammel Compton who sold it to Bernie Siegel. Roger Hayden purchased the building and opened Ray's Home Center. At various points in time the building was also used as the teen club dance hall and the Men's Pitch Club also played cards here. In 1984 it was purchased by Mr. and Mrs. Mariano de la Puente for a feed store. The building was demolished in 1986 and the Leonardo's Pizza restaurant was built on the site. A small house was located next to the mill and occupied by Sadie Hempstone Handley, Isaac and Edna Cubitt, Raymond and Lucie Beall, and Marion and Helen Beall. This house was later torn down.

85. Walter House

This two-story frame house was occupied by Mrs. Elias Moulden in 1865, and later by William Walter who had a wheelwright and blacksmith shop nearby. All three buildings are indicated on the 1879 Atlas of Montgomery County. Other occupants include Doc Louden, Mr. and Mrs. Dave Ward, Mr. and Mrs. C. R. Bodmer, Mr. and Mrs. Charles Kohlhoss, Mr. and Mrs. Charles Stone, Mr. and Mrs. Gorman Butler, Mr. and Mrs. Joseph Remsburg, Mr. and Mrs. Owen Remsburg and the Yates family. The building was demolished after it was sold to St. Peter's Episcopal Church and the space is now used for extra parking.

86. Darby-Fyffe-Chiswell House

This house was built in 1912 by Charles Sellman for Mr. and Mrs. James Washington Darby to spend their retirement years. Mr. Darby was a retired miller, who missed operating his mill and had another one built next door. The one and a half story frame house has a decorative center gable and two chimneys. The front porch is supported by four columns, and the Victorian bays windows flank the sides of the house. It was later occupied by Isaac and Elizabeth Dade Darby Fyffe. Their daughter, Mrs. Mary Fyffe Chiswell married Carroll Chiswell and still lives here. She was the granddaughter of Mr. and Mrs. James Darby.

87. Summerville House

Bill Summerville and his family lived in a frame structure that has been gone since 1927. Mr. Summerville was a handyman and rang the bell for services at St. Peter's Episcopal Church. The building had been part on the Frederick Sprigg Poole property. On Westerly Road Tuck Summerville lived in a house next to the Harvey White farm. He brewed his own beer and kept it down in a well.

88. Davis-Hersberger House

This one and a half story frame house was built in 1916 for Mr. and Mrs. Horace
Davis. Their daughter, Mrs. Edna Earle Davis Hersberger, conveyed it to her son
Marshall Davis Hersberger and his wife Marian Gladys Garrett Hersberger. Roy
and Frances Selby purchased the house and lived here for a number of years.
Rebecca Selby Brooks is the present owner. The house was remodeled to include
two apartments.

89. John Henry Williams Farm

This property on Westerly Road previously had another house, as the foundation is still visible. The present house was built for John Williams. The house is a two and a half story, three-bay frame building with double chimneys. The full length front porch is emblished with jigsaw cornices. The log outbuildings date to the early part of the Nineteenth Century. The land was parceled from the White farm after the marriage of Sarah White to John Williams. Their daughter Elizabeth was born in the house in 1870. Later Will Thomas owned the farm and it was run by tenant farmers Arthur and Grace Matthews, and Charles Munday. John Offutt and his brother-in-law Linwood T. Jones were the subsequent owners. Raymond B. "Happy" Poole later farmed for Dr. Andrews who sold the property to Ed Schram.

90. Stoney Castle

Surveyed for Robert Peter on May 17, 1784 this tract was "Resurvey on Part of Forest" containing 1,796 acres. George Peter conveyed a portion of the land to Thomas Fletchall for $4,780 in 1818. Robert P. Dunlop, a trustee for James Fletchall probably had the first section of the house built c. 1800. In 1831 the land was conveyed to Stephen Newton White. The main section of the house was probably built in this vintage of locally quarried stone. The five bay, two and a half story house has two end chimneys, and a center two story porch supported by six columns. Stephen Newton White had married Mary Veirs on December 2, 1824 and in 1831 they brought their three children to their new home, where their fourth child was born on August 29, 1832. They named him Elijah Veirs White later known as Colonel "Lige" White. In 1862 the property passed to his brother Benjamin White who removed a portion in the rear of the house. In 1908 his son Harvey Jones White inherited the property and in 1933 deeded the 330 acres property to his son Dr. Byron Dyson White. During Dr. Byron and wife Matilda White's ownership the facilities were modernized and the home was remodeled. The oldest section houses the colonial kitchen and pantry which retain the fireplace with its' crane for kettles. Formal gardens grace the back of the home. In 1949 the property was sold to Madeleine Kneppelhout van de Sterkenburg, the former Countess de Chastel of Belgium, and her husband Cornelius. Their daughter, Marie-Renee and husband Alfred W. Spates presently live here.

91. Broad Run Meeting House

Benjamin White donated the acre of land for the building which was constructed in 1876. The congregation may have been meeting prior to this as William Melvin, a 90 year old Old School Baptist Clergyman is listed in Poolesville in the 1850 census. This "Old School" Baptist Chapel on a stone foundation was frame with four windows on each side. The vestibule also had a window on each side topped with a belfry with four windows and a bell tower which had beautiful cornice work and a steeple. In the rear of the building a small frame addition was constructed. The church was dedicated on May 30, 1909 and the lake on the grounds were used for baptismal services. This congregation was not associated with the Poolesville Baptist Church. One of the weddings held here was of Mary E. White daughter of Benjamin F. and Charlotte E. Kilgour White to Honore M. Claggett son of the Honorable John Claggett in September of 1889. The officiating minister was Elijah Veirs White. The building was torn down after 1963 and a residence is located on the old foundation.

92. Williams-Allnutt House

The four-bay stone house was c. 1814 for Richard Walter Williams and his wife Hester Chiswell White Williams. Stephen Newton Chiswell Williams and his wife Sarah Randolph Hall Williams lived here in the 1870's. When Lucie Williams married Joseph NewtonAllnutt the house passed into the Allnutt family. Their sons, Richard Walter and Kenneth, inherited the house. A frame addition was removed more recently and the house retained it's original charm.

93. Locust Grove Farm

The Zachariah Williams house stood here in the 1860's. During the Civil War Camp Benton was built here and the home fell into a state of disrepair by 1870. There was a firing range located west of the house, and the encampment was spread throughout the fields. Instead of repairing the house, it was torn down, and the present house was built in 1876 for Charles McGill and Prudence Jane Waters Williams. The two and a half story, three-bay frame house has an addition on the back. The Williams raised cattle, chickens, barley, wheat, corn, and other crops here. The chinked log meat house is well preserved and dates from this period. The stones in the family cemetery were moved to Monocacy Cemetery in Beallsville. The house was inherited by Dr. Rodger Walter Williams and his brother Dorsey. Rodger Jr. inherited his Uncle Dorsey's half of the farm and purchased the remainder from his father in the late 1960's. Presently Mary Shaw Brown Williams resides in this home.

94. Maple Heights

Built in 1905 for Harvey Joners White, this two and a half story, five-bay, frame house is set back at the end of a tree lined lane. The front porch spans the entire length of the house and the half-round in the center gable distinguishes the house from the others in the vicinity. Harvey was the son of Benjamin and Sarah E. Jones White who owned Stoney Castle. He lost an eye and several fingers fighting Indians in the West. He was married three times and served two terms in the Maryland House of Delegates. The house was sold to Charles Jamison in 1950.

95. Davis-Fisher House

Prior to 1783 this property was part of "Difficulty" owned by George Willson. The tract was resurveyed in 1765 for 231 acres. It was deeded to James Soper in 1783 with a log house and three out buildings. The log section of the house was added on to and the present two-story house has a wrap-a-round porch, central chimney and a chimney in the ell. Thomas Carr Lannan purchased this 90 acre parcel in 1842 for $405. He also purchased 93 acres from the adjoining land "Resurvey on Part of Forest" from Peter's heirs. Daniel Heffner purchased the property in 1847 and sold it in 1859 to Elizabeth A. Offutt for $3,500. Elizabeth married Raphael T. Jarboe and lived here until selling the 146 acres to Horace Anderson and William Viers Bouic, Jr. for $4,400 on December 4, 1873. George C. and Sarah Agnes Fisher bought the property at auction for $5,017. In 1878 they granted it to Charles C. and Julia K. Maught who divided the land in 1881 selling 103 acres to Charles W. and Annie E. Bartgis. Isaac Fyffe bought the remaining 44 acres. The next owners, Frank I. and Susie Davis, hired Charles Sellman to add a kitchen, breakfast room, and pantry with bedrooms over them and a cellar under them with a Delco generator for electricity. Susie taught piano lessons and played for the silent movies in Poolesville. Frank became the clerk of the circuit court and sheriff of Montgomery County. In 1945 the house was sold to Carl T. and Ruth F. Fisher. During the 1960's and 70's the house had several owners and then was vacant. The house was purchased in 1984 by Robert J. and Patricia C. Pierce who are restoring the house.

96. Poolesville School

The first building on this site was a two-story frame schoolhouse constructed at a cost of $3,234 between January 1905 and January 1906. The property was purchased from Edward and Betty Wootton for $410 and was two acres, three rods and two perches. Classes met in the former Y. M. C. A. building during the construction of the school, which had previously held classes in the one-room school house described on page 85. Robert W. Stout had served as the principal there since 1904 and in 1906 his annual salary was $489.50. The new school furniture and equipment cost $171.58 and and additional $102 was spent for incidentals. The school was a direct result of the efforts of DeWalt J. Willard and Rev. Samuel Richardson White. Outlying one-room schoolhouses, and in the case of Horse Pen School, which had been meeting in a rented room, were being consolidated during this period. Mr. Willard, the school commissioner and resident of the Poolesville area knew first hand how desperately the new school was needed as he had previously rented the room the Horse Pen scholars. He convinced the School Board to build this and other schools in Montgomery County. The teachers in 1906 were Miss Emma Williams, Miss Betty Griffith and Mrs. Magruder Viers. Grades 1-7 attended classes with an enrollment of 89 students but an average attendance of 61. One of the schools that closed that year was Union School, located southwest of town, sending its' 16 students to Poolesville via a horse drawn wagon. In 1907 Cedar Bend School at Sycamore Landing also closed, sending the students to Poolesville. In 1910 grades 8 and 9 were added were added to the curriculum.

This photograph taken in 1909 shows principal Robert W. Stout on the left. He was the principal from 1906-1921. Lying down: James Brooks, Baker Selby, Arthur Mobley; first row: Carl Fisher, Charles Kohlhoss, Carroll Pyles, Jack Handley; second row: Matthew Kohlhoss, Minter Stout, Frankie Anderson, Henry Baker, Carroll Chiswell, Malcolm Handley, Archie Handley, Bryan Yates, Mannie Bodmer, Russell Baker, John Oxley, Henry Josiah Norris; third row: Florence Brooks, Thelma Pyles, Christine Kohlhoss, Rebecca Stout, Mary Fyffe, Carolyn Williams, Catherine Fisher, Blanche Griffith, Marie Chiswell, Mary Ellen Norris, Ernestine Kohlhoss, Rebecca Griffith, Ella Wooton, Beulah Brooks, LaRue Norris, Grace Wise, Virginia Gott; fourth row: Edward Beatty, Willie Magruder, Byron Chiswell, Robert Hempstone, Ralph Williams, Jennings Selby, Lena Yates, Irene Bosley; fifth row: Robert Stout, principal; Jessie Bodmer, Marguerite Kohlhoss, Lulu Mae Chiswell, Genevieve Mossburg, Effie Selby, Loretta Offutt, Ruth Beall, Minnie Brooks, Elsie Fink, Clarine Fletchall, teacher; Betty Griffith, teacher.

In 1911 the first horse drawn school bus in the state of Maryland was transporting children to Poolesville Grammar School. It was driven by Lloyd Grubb. Other schools had wagons prior to this time that were used twice a day for this purpose, but this was the first exclusive vehicle dedicated to the transportation of students, and designed for this use. In 1914 grade 10 was added. The school was originally built to hold 35-40 students and 125 were now attending classes. Paul Calvert Cissel, the first vocational agriculture teacher, had limited space for his classes during these years. The following year grade 11 was added and Thomas W. Pyle became the principal. A two-story addition with two classrooms and an assembly hall was built in 1922-23 of red clay brick. It adjoined the original building which received an additional window on each floor and brick veneering to match the addition. Two small schools closed in 1923 sending their students to Poolesville: Dawsonville and Marble Quarry near Martinsburg. C. S. Fields was paid $17.00 for transporting the Marble Quarry students to Poolesville. The gymnasium and auditorium building measuring sixty-five by thirty-seven feet was constructed behind the school in 1925 and during construction some classes met in buses in the parking lot. Eight teachers taught the 275 pupils which now included students from Sugarland School which closed that year. Mr. Pyle left in 1926 and Raymond Blackwell assumed the leadership of the school. He was succeeded by B. O. Aiken who was followed by D. A. Dollarhide. In 1929 the Montgomery County Board of Education purchased two acres for future expansion which adjoined the school campus. Elmer School at Oak Hill closed in 1930, which again increased the enrollment. In 1933 the twelfth grade was added and a one-story addition with two classrooms was built behind the gymnasium.

The Poolesville School Soccer Team from 1919 is pictured below.   Front row:
Bill Moore, Jim Brooks, Carl Haller; second row: Harold Hildebrand, Mel
Myerly; and standing: Bill Burner, Frank Roberts, Arthur C. Elgin, Bill Trundle,
Wallace Poole, and Charles Loy.

The photograph below was taken c. 1920 and shows Poolesville School with Miss Molly Green and her students. Front row: James Titus, Ralph Cubitt, Marion Beall, George Orrison; second row: Elsie Titus, Mildred Fawley, Virginia Beall, Katie Beall, Cindy Titus, Carrie Beall, Melissa Beall; third row: Miss Molly Green, Ruby Cubitt, Edna Beall, Nellie Beall, Marion Beall, Jr.; back row: Kathleen Titus, Elizabeth Beall, Anna Beall, Bob Fawley.

Also taken in the 1920's the following students have been identified: Starting in the front row on the left 6-Billy Williams, 10-Charles Sellman, 11-Perry Griffith, 12- Leonard Jewel, 13-Joe Darby, 15 Theodore Young, 16- George Brewer, 17-Harold Brooks, 18-Gordon Darby, 21-William Wootton, 25-Boyd Brooks. Second row: 26-Jack Elgin, 37-Margaret Griffith, 41-Irene Darby, 45-George Roberts. Row three: 55-Doris Bodmer, 56-Louise Hersperger, 57-Mary Martin Clagett, 58-Elizabeth White, 60-Helen Norris, 62-Louise Grubb, 63-Louise Kohlhoss, 64-Emma Haller, 65-Annabel Rutherford, 74-Dorothy Wootton. Row Four: 82-Maggie Fox, 83-Matilda Fox, 85-Ruth Beall, 86-Virginia Poole. Row Five: 97-Lester Beall, 99-Mildred Grubb, 101-Dorothy Morningstar, 102-Esther Grubb, 103 Virginia Fyffe, 104-Catherine Fisher, 105-Hilda Fyffe, 106-Helen Oland, 107-Arthur Elgin, 110-Catherine Hall, 111-Miss Burke. Row Six: 112-E. Guy Jewel, 113-Elsie Brooks, 114-Margaret Myerly, 115-Reno Darby, 117-Connie Chiswell, 118-Mildred Chiswell, 119-Evelyn Darby Allnutt. On the following page are two photographs taken in the mid-1920's. The top one is students of Mrs. Ruth Compher and the lower one is the students of Miss Olivia Green.

This photograph of the students at Poolesville was taken c. 1927. The front row has Annie Waddell, Evelyn Cubitt, Pauline Elkins, Mary White, Hazel Wood, Ellen Poole, Ida Wynne, Snow Childress, Nina Pennington, and Elizabeth Norris; row two: Ruth Young, Mary Crabtree, Estelle White, Carolyn Hickman, ?, Hazel Hickman and Ethel Darby; row three: Edwin D. Cruit, Dunbar Darby, Adele Lydanne, Clara Painter, Lena Jones, Virginia Ball, Dick Sellman, and Martz Zimmerman; row four: ?, Jimmie Allnutt, ?, Edgar Shawver, Kyle Ruble, Charles W. Elgin, Harry Fyffe, Horace Hersberger, Garnett Ball, and Mary Ethel Garner White.

In 1938 the Comus Schoolhouse was moved to Poolesville's campus and remodeled to house the home economics class. Laborers from the Works Projects Administration [WPA] built a one-story cinderblock and brick veneer building for the primary grades in 1939 and the older building was remodeled to include the cafeteria, library and shower rooms. Two additional classrooms were added to the Primary School the following year. In November the School Board purchased five more acres for expansion which contained a barn. The vocational agriculture classes used the barn for their animal experimental feeding program. In 1941 a vocational building was constructed for the farm shop students and agricultural classes. Principal C. M. Wilson resigned in 1945 and Miss Olivia Green finished out the school term in that capacity. Robert Skaife was the principal in 1945-46.

Harry C. Rhodes served as the principal from 1947-52. Another building program began during these years which was completed in 1958. Pictured below are the elementary teachers: [back row] Helen Pumphrey, Ruth Compher, Ara Lee Jones, Mary Ethel White, Shirley Youngerman, Al Evans, [front row] Agnes Fuller, Mary Reynolds, Marian Byerly, Mary Elgin, Virginia Hersperger. The secondary teachers: [back] Maurice Ward, Walter Downs, Elam Suplee, Al Sudasky, Frank Coburn, Harry Rhodes, [front] Kathryn Phipps, Olivia Green, Marion Waters, Betty Rose, Ruth Fisher, Emma Crist, and Frances Fausold.

Thomas W. Pyles, a PHS alumni, became principal in 1953. When the School Board considered closing Poolesville's schools and sending the students to Gaithersburg and Rockville a meeting was held and residents turned out en mass demanding expansion, not closure. Robert T. Crawford was the principal during integration. In 1958, with and enrollment of 668 students, the High School's third addition was built. It included a new gymnasium, library, home economics department, science department, and additional office space. The original building was razed and the Comus building sold and removed.

97. Gray House

This two-story, three bay, Colonial Revival frame house was built in 1918 for Robert and Margaret Williams Gray after their marriage. They had three children Carolyn, G. Robert, Jr. and Harry who became an obstrician. The house was continuously occupied by the Gray family until 1990. The currently owners are Mr. and Mrs. Jack F. Douglas.

98. Methodist Episcopal Church

The Methodist Episcopal congregation was formed in this area as a class in 1816. When sufficient numbers were reached to become part of the circuit a church was built. The land for the church was donated by Major George Peter on May 15, 1820. The parcel was part of "Forest" and sold to Trustees Nathaniel E. Magruder, John Douglas, Martin Fisher, Thomas Green, Jr., Dennis Lackland and George B. Hays. The church was completed in 1826 and the first pastor was Reverend Thomas W. Green. Reverend Green was later buried beneath the pulpit of the church in 1833. Some of the pastors during this period were Reverend Hempfield, Reverend John A. Collins, Reverend Horace Holland, Reverend John W. Stout, Reverend Brown, Reverend E. E. Shipley, Reverend William Hank, Reverend Robert Bean, Reverend John Lanhan, Reverend John L. Gilbert, Reverend Joseph Phelps, Reverend D. M. Browning, and Reverend Balaska. The need for a Methodist Episcopal cemetery was answered in 1839 with the interment of Ruth Eagle. By 1856 there were sixty-four members of the Poolesville Methodist Sunday School Class. Following the Civil War twenty-four members broke away to form the Methodist Episcopal Church South in 1866. Among them were Frederick Young, George Houghs, William Houghs and John O. Merchant. The first pastor of the Methodist Episcopal Church Shouth was Reverend John P. Hall and the members worshipped in the Poolesville Baptist Church until their new building was completed at a cost of $1,500. The brick building was dedicated in 1868 by Elder Samuel Register of the Baltimore Conference. The first pastor to serve in the new brick church was the Reverend Robert Smith and Rufus Wilson was the junior preacher. As Poolesville residents were largely Southern sympathizers, the membership grew to fifty during the post-war years. In 1871 the Montgomery Circuit was redistricted to include Poolesville. In 1892 the congregation considered repairing the old church, or building a new one. The congregation voted to construct a new building on Elgin Road. The two front windows were bricked in as was the large two-story arched rear window. The red brick building was later painted white. On September 2, 1892 a chapter of the Y. M. C. A. purchased the property from the heirs of George Peter and various groups used the building for social affairs such as plays and dances. Black musician Steve Williams often played for the dances. He was known far and wide for his skill as a fiddler. For many years national, state and county elections were held here. Masonic meetings were also held here for a time. On January 31, 1896 the building The Poolesville Town Hall Association purchased the building. In 1905-1906 classes were taught by Miss Mary Fyffe in this building while the new public school was under construction. Another short-lived venture was that of Harry Rhodes, showing movies here. The Poolesville Band practiced here for a time and St. Peter's Episcopal Sunday School and Church nursery was also held here before they built additional facilities. The building has also been used as the

Poolesville Drug Store, Veterinary Office, and the Poolesville Thrift Store. The Pastors serving the Methodist Episcopal Church South:

John P. Hall   1866
Robert Smith   1868
  Rufus Wilson, assistant
Benjamin F. Ball 1870
Rev. Tibbs   1872
Wade McDonald 1874
William Wade   1875
  L. L. Lloyd, assistant
Rev. Gover   1877
  D. L. Blakemore
  James H. Boyd
W. W. Watts   1880
  Rev. Sanders
  Cortland P. Smith assistant
William Hammond 1890

98. Poolesville One-Room School site

The first school in Poolesville was located in the Seymour House, but as the community grew, a school facility was needed. This parcel of "Part of Forest" was conveyed from Major George Peter's widow Sarah N. Peter to the Trustees of Poolesville School on July 27, 1841. The Trustees were: Frederick Sprigg Poole, Thomas Carr Lannan, Thomas R. Hall, Richard P. Spates, Hezekiah Trundle, William Cissel, Jonathan B. Benson, Elias Spalding, William Poole, William Matthews, and Gerhart Metzger. The provisions included that "Vacancies on the Board are to be filled by the subscribers to the school so that said Board shall always be eleven members." The one-room school was built in 1841. It operated as a pay school, and the parents or "subscribers" contributed $12.50 per quarter, per student. The first teacher was Mr. Herbert who was followed by Hilleary T. Jarvis. Textbooks cost 12 1/2 cents per year and were rented to students. Teachers during the 1850's included: James P. B. Hanks and Robert J. Groff. The school masters in the 1860's were John P. Bouic, R. W. Saunders, Joseph Dyson, Thomas Carr Lannan, Samuel S. Hays, and Ezekial Hughes. In 1862-65 the teacher was John William Booth, who was also the pastor of the Baptist Church. The Baptist congregation met in this school house from 1863-1872. In 1869 Sallie G. Collinson was the teacher. Principals of this school include: Mr. Baggerly, Silas Davis, and then Robert Stout who came in the fall of 1904. This school was sold in 1904 to Julius Hall for $525 who stored a horse drawn hearse and other things for his funeral and undertaking business. He was an associate of William Hilton of Barnesville.

99. Fletchall Farm House

Located outside of the corporate limits of Poolesville, lies the Fletchall Family Farm which was purchased from William Poole on January 14, 1860. These fifty seven acres were part of "Flint's Grove". The house was built for Captain John Thomas and Mary Thomsey Poole Fletchall in 1860. Martin and Genevieve Mossburg Wise owned and occupied the house for a number of years. Thomas and Laura Conlon purchased the house and later sold it to Charles H. and Laura Conlon Jamison. It is currently occupied by Bill's Lawn Mowing Business.

100. Old Chiswell Place

This Eighteenth Century farmhouse was built c. 1778 for George Frazier Magruder. Colonel Thomas Fletchall purchased the log home in 1804 and willed it
to his daughter Sarah and her husband William Chiswell in 1819. The frame
portion of the house was built by their son George Walter Chiswell who formed
the Poolesville Civil War unit known as "Chiswell's Exiles." These men with
additional recruits from the area became Company B of the 35th Battalion
Virginia Cavalry. The Federal style portion of the house is two-story and features
a living room, hall, bedrooms, and staircase. The Historic Medley District
purchased the house and remodeled it to show the value of restoring historic
homes. In danger of demolition, it was saved in 1975 with funding from the
Maryland Historic Trust. Presently situated on six and three-quarters acres, the
our buildings include the stone spring house, log meathouse, barn, and a log shed.
sold it to Mr. and Mrs. Leonard Dill in 1978. It is presently owned by Robert D.
and Holly Simmon.

101. Joseph Poole House

"Poole's Hazard" was built for John Poole, Sr. on seventy acres of "Elizabeth's Delight" in 1769. The two story brick house is three bays with a center door. The right wing was constructed at a later date. Additional acreage was purchased enlarging the property to 158 acres. William Poole left this to his son Thomas H. Poole, who left it to his daughter Ann Elizabeth Poole Hempstone and her husband Vernon Hempstone. On August 19, 1919 it was deeded to Samuel B. Milford who lived there until it was purchased by Warren and Marguerite Irwin. The photograph was taken in 1951. The house is currently owned and occupied by Patricia Croker.

BIBLIOGRAPHY

A Grateful Remembrance, Hiebert and MacMaster, MCHS, 1978

Atlas of Montgomery County, Md., C. M. Hopkins, 1879

Baltimore Sun, May 28, 1941, Roger McKinsey

Briarley Hall School Catalog, 1918

Circling Historic Landscapes, Maryland-NCPPC, 1980

Civil War Guide to Montgomery County, Maryland, Charles Jacobs, 1983

Development of Poolesville Schools, Dr. Harry C. Rhodes, 1978

Genealogical Companion to Rural Montgomery County Cemeteries,
Dona Cuttler, Heritage Books, 2000

History of Comus, Dona Cuttler, Heritage Books, Inc., 1999

History of Elijah United Methodist Church and Cemetery, Irene C. Pierce,
Historic Medley District, 1995

History of Hyattstown, Dona Cuttler, Heritage Books, Inc., 1998

History of Montgomery County, T. H. S. Boyd, 1879, Clearfield, 1996

History of Western Maryland, Scharf 1910

Interviews with Ida Lu Brown, 1999

Interview with Tom Brown, December 1999

Interviews with Mary Fyffe Chiswell, 1999

Interviews with Dorothy Elgin, 1999

Interview with Frank Jamison, December 1999

Interviews with Doris Matthews Lewis, 1999

Interview with James Poole, 1999

Interview with Dr. Harry Rhodes, December 1999

Interview with Mary Shaw Brown Williams, December 1999

Montgomery Circuit Records 1788-1988, Dona Cuttler, Heritage Books, Inc. 2000

Montgomery County Deeds Liber STS folio 4, 378

Montgomery County Deeds BS 6, folio 98

Montgomery County Deeds STS 3, folio 670

Montgomery County Judgement Records, Liber BS 11, folio 463

Montgomery County Land Records, Liber BS 6, folio 98

Montgomery County Land Records, Liber EBP 1, folio 200

Montgomery County Land Records, Liber EBP 5, folio 240

Montgomery County Land Records, Liber EBP 12, folio 75

Montgomery County Land Records, Liber EBP 30, folio 14

Montgomery County Land Records, Liber I, folio 370

Montgomery County Land Records, Liber JA 3, folio 65

Montgomery County Land Records, Liber JA 7, folio 84

Montgomery County Land Records, Liber JA 34, folio 316

Montgomery County Land Records, Liber JA 53, folio 6

Montgomery County Land Records, Liber JGH 8, folio 648

Montgomery County Land Records, Liber K, folio 133
Montgomery County Land Records, Liber M, folio 245
Montgomery County Sentinel, August 11, 1855
Montgomery County Sentinel, January 11, 1878
Montgomery County Sentinel, August 8, 1890
Montgomery County Sentinel, December 26, 1902
Montgomery County Sentinel, September 1, 1905
Montgomery County Sentinel, December 22, 1911
Montgomery County Story, Volume V, Number 1, page 6,
        Roger S. Cohen, Jr., 1961
Montgomery County Story, Volume 21, No. 4, p. 2,
        Charles and Marian Waters Jacobs
Montgomery County Story, Volume 26, No. 2, p. 51, Mary Charlotte Crook
Poolesville, A Brief History, Commissioners of Poolesville,
        E. E. Halmos, Jr. 1970
Poolesville Memorial Methodist Church, Zada and Charles Rozier Bodmer, 1967
Poolesville Presbyterian Church Pamphlet
Prince George's Heritage, Louise Joyner Hienton,
        Garamond/Pridemark Press, 1972
Rockville Maryland Journal, September 8, 1849
Schools That Were, E. Guy Jewell, unpublished manuscript
Twentieth Regiment of Massachusetts Volunteer Infantry
        by George A. Bruce, 1906
United Daughters Of The Confederacy, E. V. White Chapter Record Book, 1912
Vestry Records of St. Peter's Church 1850-1900
35th Battalion Virginia Cavalry, Second Edition, H. E. Howard, 1985
        John E. Divine

INDEX

Bliss, Bill, 38, 76
Bob's Bikes, 76
Bodmer, Carrie, 114, Charles Rozier,
31, 39, 113, Doris, 160, Jacob, 26,
34, 39, 113, 114, 118, 130, Jessie,
156, Mannie, 156, Mollie, 112,
Mrs., 144, Roy, 112, Zada, 113
Bogle, G., 69
Bolinger, Warren, 5
Booth, John, 76, 105, 169
Bosley, Irene, 156
Boswell, William, 13
Bouic, John, 13, 22, 169, William, 154
Boyd, James, 168
Boyer, C., 36
Boyles, Charles, 13
Bozzell, William, 13
Brace, Russell, 5, 6
Braddock, Williams, 13
Brady, Edward, 13
Brander, Archey, 26
Brault, Y., 38
Breathard, John, 13
Brenneman, Joseph, 78
Brewer, Bettie, 107, George, 18, 41, 84,
107, 160, Nicholas, 5,
William, 3, 5, 41
Briarley Hall, 40, 42, 44, 45, 49, 108,
133
Broad Run Meeting House, 150
Brookeville, 73
Brooks, Beulah, 156, Boyd, 160,
Elsie, 160, Estelle, 140, Harold, 140,
160, James, 156, Jim, 100, 158,
Kathryn, 138, Lewis, 138, Minnie,
156, Rebecca, 147, Thomas, 53,
W., 53
Broome, Mary, 43
Brown, Herbert, 36, 143, Malcolm, 38,
Neal, 38, R. 36, Reverend, 167,
Richard, 36, T., 110
Browning, D., 167, Silas, 39, 121

Brunswick, 11
Brunhard, James, 13
Brusnan, John, 13
Buchanan, James, 91
Buck Lodge, 143
Burch, Francis, 22
Burdette, Gary, 36
Burke, Miss, 160
Buner, Bill, 158
Business High School, 49
Butler, Charles, 13, 17, 22, George, 13,
17, 22, Gorman, 38, 144, Mr., 114,
William, 97
Butterball, William, 55
Butz, Thompson, 36
Buxton, Mary, 107
Byerly, Marian, 164
Byrd, John, 18

C & O Canal, 1, 4, 7, 20, 142
Calhoun, George, 13
Callahan, Catherine, 84, Daniel, 84
Camp Benton, 8, 9, 10,
Campbell, Aeneas, 2, 3, 65, C., 62,
Fred, 118, Henrietta, 65, James, 2,
Jessie, 118, Lafon, 37
Cangiano, James, 36
Cantwell, Michael, 13
Carey, John, 18
Carlisle, David, 7, 13, 22, James, 36,
William, 13
Carroll, Daniel, 1, 82, 83, 84, Eleanor,
83, Elizabeth, 83, Mary, 83
Casale, A., 134
Casale's Barbershop, 134
Cassedy, Miller, 46
Catlett, Grandison, 3
Cator, Benjamin, 5, 6, 18, Joseph, 26,
Samuel, 5, 25, 39, 40, 119, 120,
139, Thomas, 18, 25, 40
Cator's Blacksmith Shop, 25, 40
Cecil, Christopher, 13

176

Green, Thomas, 167, William, 14
Griffith, Berkley, 34, Betty, 155, 156,
  Blanche, 156, Elizabeth, 70,
  Howard, 18, 41, Margaret, 160,
  Perry, 160, Rebecca, 156, Sallie, 43,
  William, 32, 36, 68, 70, 127
Griffiths, B., 88
Griggs, Sallie, 89, Walter, 88, 89
Grimes, Charles, 26, 41, John, 26
Groff, Robert, 5, 169
Ground Hogs, 131
Grubb, Bessie, 72, Catherine, 117,
  Esther, 160, Ethel, 106, Henry, 1, 2,
  James, 70, John, 70, Lloyd, 117,
  157, Louise, 160
Guthrie, Lawrence, 112, Mary, 112,
  Mildred, 160

Hagerstown, 83
Hall, B., 53, Beulah, 112, Catherine,
  160, Cincinnatus, 6, 18, 25, Clara,
  99, Dora, 34, 130, E., 41, John, 5, 6,
  18, 26, 27, 40, 51, 78, 91, 130, 167,
  168, Joseph, 5, 25, Julius, 7, 59, 78,
  96, 169, June, 135, Madeline, 125,
  Margaret, 78, Mrs., 25, 34, Rebecca,
  34, 130, Richard, 2, 83, 84, Thomas,
  5, 18, 20, 24, 25, 40, 41, 60, 112,
  130, 134, 169
Hall's Tin Shop, 25
Haller, Carl, 158, Emma, 160,
  Gertrude, 67, Joseph, 67
Halmos, Eugene, 38, 67
Hamill, Henry, 69
Hammond, Will, 168
Hampton, Wade, 21
Hancock, Winfield, 21
Hand Made'ns Gift Shop, 129
Handley, Archie, 156, Malcolm, 156,
  Sadie, 143
Hank, William, 167
Hanks, James, 169

Harbin, Jeremiah, 3
Harding, Abraham, 14, B., 74, Josiah,
  2, Lloyd, 3
Hardy, James, 26
Harper, Beulah, 37
Harper's Ferry, 12, 19
Harris, Reverend, 37
Harrison, Ernest, 69
Harrison's Island, 10
Hartley, William, 14
Harwood, Thomas, 14, William, 14
Hatcher, Joshua, 6, R., 105
Hathorne, Mark, 53
Hauck, Betty, 120, Paul, 120
Hayden, Roger, 143
Hays, George, 167, Nathan, 40,
  Richard, 14, 22, Samuel, 14, 169,
  William, 26, 41
Hayward, Kathleen, 87, Stephen, 87, 89
Hearthside Antiques Store, 105
Henderson, George, 14, John, 13,
Heffner, [Heifner], Christian, 25, 26,
  Daniel, 6, 7, 21, 79, 154,
  Stephen, 14
Heintzelman, Samuel, 18
Heiberg, Alfred, 76, 87, 120, Louise,
  76, 87, 120
Heister, Ronald, 89
Hempfield, Reverend, 167
Hempstone, Ann, 79, 172, Christian, 3,
  79, H., 41, Lutie, 111, Mary, 79,
  Robert, 6, 76, 79, 156, T., 41,
  Vernon, 79, 172
Herbert, John 15, Mr, 169, William, 15
Hersberger, Aaron, 41, Horace, 162,
  Marian, 147, Marshall, 147
Hersperger, Louise, 160, S., 49,
  Virginia, 122, 164
Hershey, David, 32
Hess, Carl, 36
Hickley, W., 15
Hickman, Carolyn, 162, Hazel, 162,

180

Hickman, John, 133, 136, 137
Higgins, Darius, 5, Jesse, 5, 8, 21,
   Joshua, 3, Richard, 3
Hildebrand, Harold, 158
Hillard, [Hilliard] George, 68, 130, 138,
   John, 18, Kathryn, 68, 130, Raymus,
   69, Robert, 18, 41
Hilton, Clagett, 32, 127, William, 36,
   88, 138, 169
Hodgson, Emma, 32, 57, 77, 117,
   Estelle, 57, 77, 117
Hoeing, Reva, 101
Hold, W., 53
Holland, George, 31, Horace, 167,
   John, 15, 22
Holmes, Oliver, 10
Hooker, Joseph, 21, Theodora, 43
Hoskins, James, 15, John, 18
Hopkinson, Nancy, 57
Horse Pen School, 155
Hoskinson, Andrew, 7, Charles, 1, 2,
   75, Dorcas, 25, 70, 91, Edward, 6,
   51, Hilleary, 5, 77, 91, Hugh, 2,
Howard, John, 3, Mary, 43, Stella, 43,
   Thomas, 34, 39, 40, 41, 69, 91,
   William, 26, 41, 69, 127
Hoskinson Brother's Store, 40, 100
Hottinger, Robert, 70
Howard, Elisha, 78
Houghes, George, 167,
   William, 17, 167
Hoyle, Nathan, 7
Hubbard, William, 15
Huerta, Hector, 37
Hughes, Adolphus, 41, Ezekial, 169,
   George, 18, Joseph, 116, Dolie, 116,
   Singleton, 53, William, 41
Hunter, John, 36
Hunton, Eppa, 10
Hyattstown, 19, 31
Hyde, Evelina, 94

IOOF, 40, 133, 134
Imirie, Fred, 67
Imlay, Laura, 117
Ingalls, Duke, 143, James, 18
Irwin, Marguerite, 172, Warren, 172
Isherwood, Isabella Darby, 42,
   Robert J., 40, 41, 42

Jackson, Brooke, 128, Miriam, 53
Jamison, Charles, 36, 92, 130, 153,
   170, Frank, 38, Laura, 170
Jamison Real Estate Company, 82
James, Thomas, 36
Janet, Stanley, 138
Jarboe, Elizabeth, 154, Eugene, 86,
   Raphael, 154, Samuel, 15
Jarvis, A., 25, E., 25, Elizabeth, 122,
   128, Hilleary, 3, 122, 169
Jenkins, Samuel, 20
Jennings, Joseph, 53
Jerusalem, 53
Jewell, E. Guy, 160, Leonard, 160
Jewett, Albert, 20
Jerusalem, 11, 53, 54
Johnny & Molly, 2
Johnson, Andrew, 38, Ann, 91,
   Bradley, 19, Edwin, 36, George, 18,
   59, Roy, 38, Thomas, 18, 51
Jones, Acshah, 70, Airy, 40, 41, 92,
   Ara, 164, Benjamin, 15, 22,
   Columbia, 92, Dolie, 43, Elizabeth,
   70, Elmer, 53, Ethel, 122, General,
   21, Isaac, 115, John, 18, 127, Lena,
   162, Linwood, 148, Lloyd, 36,
   Louis, 55, Nathan, 41, Priscilla, 115,
   140, Sarah, 115, R., 40, Richard, 4,
   41, Robert, 3, Thomas, 115,
   William, 2, 18, 41, 70, 76
Jordan, McKinley, 53
Joseph's Choice, 1, 51
Joyner, H., 49
Jukes, Herbert, 88

McLeod, Alice, 82, Wilfred, 82
McNair, R., 62
McNamara, David, 117, Kathleen, 117
McNeil, Henry, 15

Madison Heights, 22
Magaha, Joseph, 15
Magruder, George, 171, Nathaniel, 167,
    W., 46, Willie, 156
Magruder Corporation, 109
Mann, Mary, 119
Mansfield, Charles, 26, William, 26
Marble Quarry School, 157
Marlow, Richard, 12, 19
Martin, Clifton, 36, Nettie, 42,
    William, 15
Martinsburg, 157
Mason, Frank, 7
Mast, Jacob, 69
Matthews, Arthur, 148, Charles, 7,
    Doris, 31, Grace, 148, Hubert, 31,
    James, 7, 15, 22, Mary, 26, Vivian,
    31, Walter, 31, William, 7, 15, 51,
    54, 59, 62, 65, 76, 82, 169
Maught, Charles, 154, Julia, 154
Maxwell, Edward, 73, 79, John, 15
Mayes, Jesse, 53
Meadowlark Inn, 36, 112, 119
Medley District, 3, 4, 17, 94, 128, 171
Meerdink, Effie, 94, George, 94
Melton, Raphael, 3, 78
Memorial United Methodist, 69
Merchant, James, 18, John, 5, 6, 25, 26,
    40, 51, 138, 167, Margaret, 138
Merchant's Hotel, 28, 102
Metcalf, Shelley, 72
Methodist Cemetery, 167
Metzger, Amanda, 87, Charles, 41,
    George, 87, Gerhart, 92, 169,
    Hannah, 62, Mrs., 40, Sarah, 87,
    William, 18, 25, 26, 39, 41, 62, 78,
    87

Michael, Charles, 69, Martha, 128
Middleton, Percy, 53
Miles, James, 18, 26, 41, 76, Myrna,
    44, Nathan, 18, Uriah, 41
Milford, Betty, 120, Thomas, 26, 41,
    Samuel, 26, 56, 58, 86, 106, 120,
    130, 172
Milford's Mill, 4
Miller, James, 17
Mills, Franklin, 69
Mobley, Arthur, 156
Moffatt, Eleanor, 43
Moiner, John, 15, 21
Molayem, Benjamin, 95, Linda, 95
Money, Charles, 122, Fannie, 100,
    Frank, 71, 122, James, 26, 40, 41,
    76, 122, Patrick, 2, 18, Rose, 41,
    122
Monocacy Cemetery, 22, 37, 138, 152
Monocacy Chapel, 88
Monocacy Lions, 36
Montgomery Circuit, 69, 167
Montgomery County, 1, 2, 4, 7, 11, 17,
    22, 37, 49, 54, 77, 154
Montgomery County Board of
    Education, 138, 155, 157, 163, 165
Montgomery County Historical Society,
    37
Montgomery County Schools, 112
Moon, E., 53, 54, Lowell, 36
Moore, Bill, 158, Filbert, 62, John, 89
Morgan, James, 69, Rev., 139
Morningstar, Dorothy, 160, Gerald, 38,
    135, June, 135, Murrel, 91, 135,
    Richard, 135
Morningstar Welding, 135
Morra, David, 38
Morris, George, 15, William, 143
Morrison, Charles, 34, 127, Fannie,
    100, James, 18, Mary, 122, 128
Mossburg, Christian, 5, Genevieve,
    156, Jesse, 29, John, 18, Mr., 54,

186